AuDHD Burnout for Women

Why You Keep Crashing, What Recovery Requires, and How to Build a Life Your Brain Can Sustain

Jordan Amor Shamar

This book is provided for general educational and informational purposes. It is not a diagnostic tool and does not replace medical care, mental health treatment, occupational advice, or emergency support.

No particular outcome is guaranteed. Readers remain responsible for deciding which suggestions are appropriate for their circumstances and for seeking qualified professional guidance before making decisions that may affect health, medication, employment, finances, or safety.

The names, examples, and scenarios in this book are composites or have been altered to protect privacy. They are included to explain common patterns and are not intended to identify, harm, or misrepresent any person, employer, organization, or service.

ISBN: 978-1-911838-02-9

Table Of Contents

Preface

Women with co-occurring autism and ADHD are often given a useful name for their experience before they are given a workable method for responding to it. Research on autistic burnout is developing, but evidence focused specifically on AuDHD women remains limited. The practical questions are already urgent: What is consuming capacity? Which costs are staying hidden? Why does rest sometimes fail to restore everyday access? What must change before another period of collapse? This book begins with those questions while remaining clear about what current research can and cannot establish.

AuDHD is an informal term for co-occurring autism and ADHD. AuDHD burnout is used in this book as a practical description of burnout shaped by the interaction of autistic and ADHD needs. It is not a separate formal diagnosis. It may involve sustained exhaustion, reduced access to everyday abilities, greater difficulty tolerating sensory input, withdrawal, and a shrinking margin for decisions or change. It also needs to be distinguished from ordinary tiredness, occupational burnout, depression, medication effects, sleep problems, hormonal changes, and physical illness.

The central difficulty is not a lack of effort. Many women respond to falling capacity by becoming more organized, more disciplined, or more determined to keep every responsibility intact. That response can hide the seriousness of the problem while adding new demands. General burnout advice may also miss the conflict inside the combined experience. Less stimulation may help an autistic need while leaving an ADHD need for interest unmet. Novelty may help initiation while increasing sensory and switching costs. Advice written for only one side of the picture can solve one difficulty and intensify another.

This book offers a structured way to examine that pattern through the Capacity Gap Map. The model compares Visible Load,

Hidden Load, Available Capacity, and Recovery Access. It helps you identify where the pressure is coming from, which costs have gone uncounted, and which practical change has the best chance of reducing harm. The chapters then apply that model to rest, food, hygiene, household tasks, work, hormonal change, relationships, masking, rebuilding, and early warning signs.

The primary audience is women who have received autism and ADHD diagnoses in adulthood, suspect they may have both, or find that the AuDHD framework accurately describes their experience. Women at different stages of diagnosis, employment, caregiving, family life, and hormonal change may use the tools differently. Partners, relatives, employers, and support professionals may also find the explanations useful, though the book speaks directly to the person managing the loss of capacity.

This is an educational handbook, not a diagnostic test or a substitute for medical or mental health care. It does not promise a complete or permanent recovery, and it does not assume that every symptom is caused by neurodivergence. New, severe, rapidly worsening, or medically unusual symptoms require appropriate professional assessment. The exercises are planning tools, not clinically validated instruments, and results will differ according to health, environment, resources, responsibilities, and available support.

The purpose of this book is to help you see the full cost of functioning, reduce preventable strain, and build a life that asks less often for collapse as the price of keeping up.

Introduction: You're Not Failing at Rest

You get through the meeting.

You answer the questions, remember the deadline, make the right facial expressions, and sound calm enough that nobody checks whether you're all right. On the way home, you stop at the supermarket because the fridge is empty. You walk through three aisles, lose track of what you came for, and leave with crackers, toothpaste, and nothing that can become dinner.

At home, your coat stays on. The kitchen light feels too bright. A message from someone you care about appears on your phone, and even reading it feels like another task you might fail. You tell yourself you'll reply after you've rested.

An hour later, you're still sitting in the same place.

From the outside, the day looked successful. The work was done. You were polite. You kept the appointment. From the inside, the day used everything.

This is the contradiction that confuses so many women. You can do the difficult thing, then lose access to something that looks much easier. You can perform under pressure and still be unable to recover from it. You can appear capable while your private life becomes smaller, messier, quieter, and harder to maintain.

The principle that runs through this book is this:

Repeated collapse is often a capacity problem before it's a motivation problem.

That distinction changes the questions you ask. Instead of asking why you can't force yourself to do more, you begin asking what the day actually cost. Instead of judging the hours you spent lying down, you look at whether the conditions that depleted you ever changed. Instead of treating every return of energy as proof that you're fully recovered, you learn to notice whether that energy lasts after you use it.

Functioning isn't the same as recovering.

The Work Still Gets Done

Burnout is easier for other people to recognize when everything stops. You miss work. You stop answering calls. The house becomes unmanageable. You can't hide what is happening.

Many women reach a serious level of depletion long before that point. The visible parts of life may continue because those parts carry consequences. You meet the client because your income depends on it. You pack the school bag because a child needs it. You answer your manager because silence could be interpreted as a problem. You attend the family event because explaining your absence feels harder than enduring the event.

The cost appears later.

Maybe you spend the evening unable to choose food. Maybe speech becomes effortful. Perhaps you cancel the one plan you were looking forward to because all the less optional demands used the capacity that would have made enjoyment possible. You may sleep for nine hours and wake feeling as though the previous day is still happening inside your body.

This pattern can create a cruel misunderstanding. Other people see the completed task and assume you had enough capacity. You see the aftermath and accuse yourself of being inconsistent.

A completed task proves that you completed the task. It doesn't prove that the task was sustainable.

Research on autistic burnout has described a pattern of long lasting exhaustion, reduced ability to function, and increased difficulty tolerating sensory input. Participants in early qualitative work connected this state with chronic stress, an imbalance between expectations and abilities, and inadequate access to support or relief (Raymaker et al., 2020). Later research using accounts posted by autistic adults found similar themes, including masking, cumulative stress, reduced functioning, and recurring burnout (Mantzalas et al., 2022).

These findings don't give us a neat medical test that can explain every crash. They do give language to a pattern described by participants and in autistic community accounts.

The task isn't the full cost.

The meeting includes the travel, the clothing, the interruption to your routine, the background noise, the effort of tracking several people at once, the decision about when to speak, the monitoring of how you sound, and the work of returning to whatever you were doing before. Dinner includes choosing, checking ingredients, tolerating smells, touching textures, timing several steps, cleaning up, and shifting from the state you were already in.

When your capacity is high enough, those hidden steps may pass without much notice. When your capacity has narrowed, each one becomes part of the bill.

A Word About AuDHD

AuDHD is an informal term for co-occurring autism and ADHD. It isn't a separate formal diagnosis. A person may receive separate autism and ADHD diagnoses while using AuDHD as practical shorthand for the combined experience (Craddock, 2026).

Research centered specifically on women diagnosed with both conditions in adulthood is still limited. Qualitative studies have described missed recognition, gendered expectations, masking, confusion before diagnosis, and autism and ADHD as sometimes contradictory and sometimes complementary (Craddock, 2024; Craddock, 2026).

You might recognize some of those contradictions.

Part of you may want a predictable plan while another part resists repetition. You may need stimulation to begin a task, then become overloaded by the stimulation around you. You may crave company, novelty, and conversation, only to discover that the social and sensory cost arrives after you get home. You may build an ambitious system during a burst of interest, then find that maintaining the system consumes more energy than the problem it was meant to solve.

This book won't ask you to choose which side is the real one.

It will help you look for arrangements that respect both. Predictable choice. Low pressure novelty. Flexible structure. Quiet that isn't empty. Stimulation that doesn't become chaos. Support that reduces effort without taking control away from you.

You don't need to fit yourself into advice written for only half of your experience.

Burnout Is Not One Test

The phrase AuDHD burnout is used throughout this book because it gives us a practical way to discuss repeated collapse shaped by interacting autistic and ADHD needs. It should not be treated as a settled diagnostic category.

Researchers have been working to define and measure autistic burnout more carefully. Early measurement work identified exhaustion, withdrawal, and cognitive overload as core features, while finding a strong association with depression and limited ability to distinguish current from past burnout (Arnold et al., 2023). A later study in a larger sample found promising reliability and construct validity for the AASPIRE Autistic Burnout Measure, although the authors called for further validation across diverse samples (Bougoure et al., 2026).

That uncertainty has practical consequences. A word can help you recognize a pattern without explaining every symptom you have.

Severe fatigue, sleep changes, concentration problems, withdrawal, irritability, reduced motivation, appetite changes, and loss of everyday functioning can occur for many reasons. Burnout may overlap with depression, anxiety, chronic pain, sleep disorders, medication effects, hormonal changes, nutritional deficiencies, or another physical health condition. New symptoms, rapid deterioration, fainting, severe weakness, major changes in sleep or appetite, or symptoms that feel medically unusual deserve professional assessment.

This book can help you organize what you have noticed. It can't diagnose the cause.

Chapter 4 will help you create a symptom timeline and prepare for a medical or mental health appointment. You don't need to wait until Chapter 4 if something feels urgent, severe, or unsafe. Seek appropriate care now and return to the book later.

There is no prize for explaining every symptom through neurodivergence.

Rest Can Miss the Problem

You may already be resting more than anyone realizes.

You decline invitations. You spend weekends at home. You lie down after work. You watch familiar programs because following a new plot feels like effort. You scroll because it asks nothing from you for a few seconds at a time. You sleep whenever sleep is available.

Then Monday arrives, and you're no more available than you were on Friday.

This can make rest feel like another thing you're doing badly. It can also lead people around you to become impatient. They see the hours on the sofa. They don't see that your phone keeps vibrating, the house remains noisy, unfinished tasks stay mentally active, work is waiting, and every period of stillness carries the fear that you should be using it to catch up.

Time without activity isn't always time without demand.

Some forms of rest reduce movement but leave decision making, sensory strain, worry, social monitoring, or unfinished responsibilities untouched. Some provide immediate escape while leaving you more overstimulated afterward. Some are genuinely restorative but too short to compete with the load that resumes as soon as you stand up.

There is another complication. An autistic need for reduced input may exist beside an ADHD need for enough interest or stimulation to stay settled. Complete silence may soothe you on one day and make you restless on another. A familiar game may help your mind stop circling, while an hour of rapid video clips may leave you tired and activated at the same time.

Rest isn't one activity. It's a change in the kind and amount of pressure reaching you.

Chapter 6 will help you build a Rest Menu for different levels of capacity. For now, notice the result rather than judging the activity. After you rest, are you slightly more able to eat, speak, decide, move, or tolerate input? Do you feel less available? Is there no clear change? You're gathering information, not awarding yourself a grade.

Recovery Starts With Visibility

The central tool in this book is the **Capacity Gap Map**.

You will learn the full method in Chapter 2. The basic idea is that burnout risk rises when your visible and hidden load repeatedly exceed your available capacity while your access to recovery remains blocked.

Visible Load includes the responsibilities that are easy to name: employment, deadlines, travel, caregiving, appointments, housework, and money problems.

Hidden Load includes effort that often goes uncounted: masking, sensory filtering, switching between tasks, uncertainty, emotional monitoring, remembering for other people, managing interruptions, and recovering from changes.

Available Capacity is the thinking, physical, sensory, communication, and emotional access you have today. It changes.

Sleep, health, hormones, environment, medication, pain, conflict, novelty, and accumulated stress can affect it.

Recovery Access is your practical ability to obtain the kind of relief that actually helps. Time matters, but so do privacy, safety, suitable sensory conditions, money, support, and freedom from interruption.

Recovery starts by making the total cost visible.

This isn't an argument for making your life as small as possible. It's a way to stop spending capacity you haven't counted and then blaming yourself when the account is empty.

A good day is evidence of access, not proof of endless capacity.

Choose Your Starting Point

You don't have to read this book in order.

If you're in immediate collapse and even this introduction is taking effort, start with Chapter 5, **Stop Digging**. It will help you sort demands into essential, delayable, delegable, and removable, then build a Minimum Viable Day.

If food, hygiene, bills, medication, or household tasks are becoming unsafe or inaccessible, go to Chapter 7, **Protect the Basics**. Use the lowest effort options first.

If you need to understand what is happening before you can act, continue to Chapter 1 and then Chapter 2. Those chapters explain the pattern and introduce the full Capacity Gap Map.

If work is the main source of damage and you need practical language quickly, go to Chapter 8, **Work Without Pretending**.

If the people around you don't understand what has changed, Chapter 10, **Share the Weight**, offers specific ways to discuss responsibility, communication, touch, plans, and reduced availability.

If you have recovered enough to worry about another crash, Chapter 13, **Catch the Crash Earlier**, will help you define your Early Warning Window and create a written response plan.

Reading out of order isn't cheating. A handbook should meet you where the problem is.

Check Where You Are Today

Take two minutes. You can write the answers, mark them mentally, or ask someone you trust to help.

Rate each area as **available**, **strained**, or **not reliably available**:

1. Eating and drinking enough to remain safe.
2. Basic hygiene and medication routines.
3. Speech, messages, and necessary communication.
4. Work, study, caregiving, or essential appointments.
5. Tolerance for light, sound, touch, movement, and other input.
6. Ability to choose, begin, stop, and switch tasks.
7. Access to rest that leaves you even slightly more able afterward.

Now choose the area with the greatest immediate consequence. Not the area that embarrasses you most. Not the area other people complain about most. The area most connected to safety, housing, income, health, or basic care.

That becomes your first reading route.

If several areas aren't reliably available, this is useful information. It may mean that advice aimed at optimization is arriving too early. Begin with stabilization, outside support, and professional assessment where needed.

You're not required to repair your entire life before lunch.

Use Less Effort Here

Every exercise in this book is optional. The tools exist to reduce confusion, not create another backlog.

You can read one section and stop. You can photograph a worksheet instead of completing it neatly. You can circle words rather than write full sentences. You can ask another person to record your answers. You can use the examples as your plan until you have capacity to personalize them. You can skip a story and go directly to the action. You can return later without starting the chapter again.

Many books quietly reward the person who can concentrate, remember, plan, write, and follow a sequence. This book is meant to remain useful when those abilities are strained.

You may also discover that understanding arrives before action. You can recognize the pattern and still be unable to change the job, the household arrangement, the financial pressure, or the relationship that keeps recreating it. That doesn't make the recognition pointless. It tells you where the Capacity Gap is being held open.

A plan can begin with one protected meal, one cancelled commitment, one written instruction at work, one hour without conversation, or one responsibility that becomes someone else's job.

Small is not the same as trivial.

What This Book Asks

This book will ask you to become more accurate about cost.

It will ask you to count the parts of a task that nobody sees. It will ask you to notice delayed consequences, not only whether you managed in the moment. It will ask you to stop using your most productive day as the standard for every day. It will ask you to separate a temporary burst of energy from durable capacity.

It won't ask you to abandon ambition.

You may want a demanding career, an active family life, close relationships, creative projects, travel, study, community, or change. The goal isn't to remove everything that costs energy. A meaningful life contains effort. The problem begins when the effort remains invisible, support remains inaccessible, and every solution depends on pushing harder.

There may be grief in seeing the pattern clearly. You may realize that some achievements were funded by your evenings, your health, your relationships, or long periods of recovery nobody counted. You may feel angry that people praised the performance and ignored the cost.

You don't have to settle those feelings before using the tools.

For today, begin with the next honest measurement.

What did the day actually cost?

Principles to Remember

You can complete a task and still be unable to recover from it.

Visible performance doesn't reveal the sensory, cognitive, social, and physical work that made the performance possible. When those costs stay hidden, you may keep planning from the wrong number.

AuDHD is useful shorthand for the interaction between autism and ADHD. It isn't a separate formal diagnosis, and burnout language should never be used to dismiss new, severe, or medically unusual symptoms.

Rest helps when it changes the pressure reaching you. Lying down while demands remain active may be necessary, but it may not be enough.

The Capacity Gap Map will help you compare Visible Load, Hidden Load, Available Capacity, and Recovery Access. You don't need to master it today.

Choose the part of the book that matches the problem in front of you. Begin with safety and basic care. Use the smallest version of each tool that gives you useful information.

Functioning isn't the same as recovering.

Chapter 1 The Kind of Tired

Beth could still present to a room of 40 people.

She could arrive with slides prepared, answer questions, and remember the names of the senior staff who needed follow-up notes. Her voice sounded steady. Her colleagues described her as organized, calm under pressure, and unusually good at noticing what everyone else had missed.

The presentation ended at four. By five, she was sitting in her car with the engine off and both hands pressed over her ears. The car park was nearly empty before she drove home.

At home, she walked past the kitchen three times. She knew she needed food, but choosing it felt inaccessible. She opened a message from her sister, read the same two sentences several times, and put the phone face down. When her partner asked whether the presentation had gone well, Beth said, "Yes." It was the only answer she could assemble.

The next morning, she returned to work.

For months, this pattern convinced Beth that nothing serious could be wrong. People who were truly burnt out didn't deliver polished presentations, she thought. They didn't remember passwords, attend dental appointments, or sound cheerful on a call. She took the moments when her abilities appeared as evidence against the moments when they disappeared.

Her mistake was understandable. She was measuring whether she could perform the task. She wasn't measuring what happened to her access afterward.

The chapter principle is simple: burnout can reduce access to an ability without removing the ability itself. A skill may still be present while the sensory, cognitive, physical, or communication access needed to use it becomes unreliable.

A hard task can remain available because it carries urgency, structure, interest, fear, or consequence. An apparently easy task may disappear because it depends on self-starting, choice, switching, sensory tolerance, or unstructured attention. Difficulty is not ranked by how simple a task looks from the outside.

Ability and Access Differ

When people say they have "lost skills" during autistic burnout, the phrase can sound permanent. Sometimes the experience is better described as lost access. You know how to cook, but the sequence won't organize itself. You know what a message means, but language won't form around a reply. You have showered thousands of times, but the changes in temperature, clothing, sound, touch, and movement now feel like too many linked events.

Early autistic burnout research identified exhaustion, loss of function, and reduced tolerance for sensory input as central features described by autistic adults (Raymaker et al., 2020). Later studies report withdrawal, cognitive difficulties, and increased disability that can affect everyday tasks; some accounts also describe changes in communication during severe periods (Arnold et al., 2023; Ali et al., 2025).

The research does not tell us that every instance of reduced function is autistic burnout. It does support the need to take changing access seriously.

Think of access as a door with several locks. Knowing how to do the task is only one lock. You may also need enough energy, a tolerable sensory setting, a clear first step, emotional room, working memory, time, and the ability to shift from whatever came before. When several locks fail at once, effort at the final door handle does little.

This distinction matters because motivation advice usually aims at the wrong lock.

"Just start" assumes the first step is visible.

"Break it down" assumes you have enough thinking access to create and hold the smaller steps.

"Use a reward" assumes the reward remains more compelling than the immediate cost.

"Do it before you sit down" assumes you can extend a demanding state without consequence.

Each suggestion can work in the right conditions. None of them proves that failure to act is a failure to care.

Urgency Can Borrow Tomorrow

For some people with ADHD, a deadline, another person waiting, or the threat of a consequence can make action easier than ordinary intention does. You may produce excellent work at the last minute, manage a family emergency, or suddenly complete six tasks because a visitor is due.

That burst can feel like recovered capacity. It may be borrowed activation.

Jade described cleaning her entire flat the night before a landlord inspection. She moved quickly for five hours, threw away rubbish, changed the bedding, scrubbed the bathroom, and answered two work emails between rooms. The next day, after the inspection went well, she could not get out of bed until late afternoon. She used the success to insult herself.

"You could do it yesterday," she thought. "So why are you being ridiculous today?"

Yesterday contained a deadline, fear, a clear finish, and visible consequences. Today contained none of those. It also contained the cost of yesterday.

The useful question is not only, "Could I do it?" Ask, "What supplied the access, and what did using it cost?"

Action Challenge: Track the Aftermath

For one week, choose three tasks you complete and record four short details:

1. What helped you begin, such as urgency, interest, fear, company, medication timing, or a clear deadline.
2. How difficult the task felt while you were doing it.
3. What became harder during the next six to 24 hours.
4. Whether the task could be repeated at the same pace without losing essential functioning.

You're not proving that the task was bad. You're learning whether the price appeared later.

The Delayed Crash

Some costs arrive immediately. Noise hurts. Speech stops. Your body becomes heavy. You need darkness or distance from people.

Other costs are delayed. You perform well on Tuesday, feel slightly tired on Wednesday, and lose most of Thursday. The gap makes cause and effect harder to see. You blame Thursday on poor discipline because Tuesday has already been filed under success.

Some costs appear only after an activity ends. This pattern is not specific to autism. Sleep loss, illness, pain, depression, medication effects, and other conditions can also create delayed or fluctuating difficulty. The pattern is information, not a diagnosis.

A helpful way to notice it is to stop evaluating activities only while they are happening.

A social event can feel enjoyable and still be expensive.

A workday can feel manageable and still be unsustainable.

Exercise can feel good and still require a level of recovery you didn't plan.

A holiday can be wanted and still contain unfamiliar food, sleep disruption, packing, travel, crowds, decisions, and broken routines.

The immediate experience and the later cost don't cancel each other.

Ruth loved her monthly book club. She spent the evening discussing a novel with people she trusted and often stayed later than planned because conversation was stimulating. The next morning, she could barely tolerate family noise. For a long time, she assumed she had to choose between "book club is good for me" and "book club drains me." The useful answer was more specific. The event gave her connection and interest, and it used social, sensory, and sleep capacity. She began leaving 30 minutes earlier and protecting the following morning from errands.

She didn't remove a valued part of her life. She stopped pretending it was free.

Different Kinds of Unavailable

Loss of access can appear in several forms. Naming the form helps you choose a better response.

Initiation loss means you can understand and want the task but cannot cross into action. The first step may feel blocked or invisible.

Sequence loss means the task becomes a cloud of steps that won't line up. Cooking, packing, paperwork, and household projects often fail here.

Switching loss means you can continue what you're already doing but cannot stop, begin something else, or return after interruption.

Language loss means speaking, writing, reading, or finding words becomes effortful. You may understand more than you can express.

Sensory access loss means the environment makes the task intolerable. The light, sound, temperature, smell, touch, movement, or body sensation may be the barrier.

Decision access loss means all options feel equal, wrong, or impossible to compare. A simple menu can become harder than a complex work problem because the work problem has rules and the menu requires preference.

These forms can overlap. You don't need a perfect label. The point is to replace "I can't do anything" with a more useful description of what is unavailable.

Action Challenge: Name the Missing Access

Choose one task that has become difficult. Complete this sentence with as little detail as possible:

"I know how to __________, but right now I don't reliably have access to __________."

Examples:

"I know how to cook, but right now I don't reliably have access to choosing and sequencing."

"I know how to answer messages, but right now I don't reliably have access to language after work."

"I know how to shower, but right now I don't reliably have access to tolerating the temperature and transitions."

The second blank points toward support. Choosing can be reduced. Sequences can be written or simplified. Language can be replaced with a prewritten message. Sensory conditions can be changed.

Shutdown Is Not the Same as Calm

A person who has become very quiet can look settled. She may not be.

During shutdown, some autistic adults describe feeling stuck, with physical or vocal immobilization and difficulty responding (Paris et al., 2025). Research on autistic meltdowns separately describes being overwhelmed by sensory, informational, social, and emotional input (Lewis & Stevens, 2023).

From the outside, shutdown may be rewarded. You stop arguing. You agree. You leave. You say "fine." You may even continue a practiced task.

Inside, the system has narrowed.

If language is unreliable, repeated questions can increase the load. “What’s wrong?” “What do you need?” “Are you angry?” “Can you answer me?” Each question asks for body awareness, interpretation, decision, language, and social reassurance.

A better low-capacity plan can be prepared before you need it. You might use a card, text shortcut, or agreed phrase such as:

“I’m overloaded. I’m safe. I need quiet and no questions for 30 minutes. I’ll contact you when speech is easier.”

The exact wording should fit your life. The value lies in removing the need to invent language during the period when language is least available.

Depression Can Coexist

Reduced interest, withdrawal, fatigue, sleep disturbance, concentration problems, hopelessness, and difficulty functioning can also occur with depression. Burnout and depression can overlap. They can intensify each other. One should not be used to dismiss the other.

There is no reliable self-test in this book that can separate every cause. If low mood lasts, you have lost interest across most areas, you feel hopeless, or you are struggling to cope, seek professional help. If you are at risk of harming yourself or cannot remain safe, seek urgent help where you live.

The need for assessment does not invalidate the AuDHD pattern. It protects you from making one explanation carry too much.

Chapter 4 will help you compare patterns more carefully. For now, keep two statements available:

“My reduced access is real.”

“I am still allowed to ask whether something else is contributing.”

Build a Burnout Sign List

Your signs may not begin with tiredness. They may begin with friction.

Food becomes narrower. Clothes become harder to tolerate. Your tolerance for conversation drops. You become more rigid about plans because there is no spare capacity for change. You make more mistakes, lose objects, cry after interruptions, or feel trapped by ordinary requests. You may become unusually productive in one narrow area while the rest of life falls away.

Create five headings on a page:

1. Body
2. Thinking
3. Sensory experience
4. Communication
5. Daily living

Under each heading, write the first changes you notice, not only the worst ones. "Jaw tight after meetings" is more useful for prevention than "unable to work." "Eating the same food for four days" may be more useful than "stopped eating properly." "Leaving messages unread" may appear before "unable to speak."

The aim is to identify your **Early Warning Window**, the period when burnout signals are present but total collapse may still be reduced.

You will build the full prevention plan in Chapter 13. Today, you're collecting the first clues.

Access tends to narrow before it disappears.

Principles to Remember

Burnout can reduce access to an ability without removing the ability itself. Knowing how to do something is only one part of being able to do it today.

Urgency, fear, interest, and consequence can temporarily bring a skill online. That burst does not tell you whether the pace is sustainable.

Measure the aftermath. The cost of an activity may appear hours or days after the activity looked successful.

Name the missing access. Initiation, sequence, switching, language, decisions, and sensory tolerance require different forms of support.

A quiet person may be overloaded rather than calm. Prepare low-language communication before you need it.

Reduced access is real. It can also overlap with depression, sleep problems, illness, medication effects, pain, and other conditions that deserve assessment.

A task can be possible and still be too expensive.

Chapter 2: Map the Capacity Gap

Carmen opened her calendar on Sunday night and saw a normal week.

Five workdays. Two school pickups. A dental appointment. Dinner with her mother. One load of laundry. A report due Friday. Nothing looked dramatic. She had managed busier weeks before.

By Wednesday evening, she was crying because the washing machine had finished.

The sound had stopped, but the wet clothes now existed as a demand. They needed to be moved, separated, dried, and remembered. Carmen stood in the hallway thinking about the laundry while her daughter asked for help with homework, her work chat continued to flash, and the extractor fan hummed in the kitchen. Her mother sent a message asking whether dinner could move from seven to six. The change was small. Carmen's body reacted as though the floor had shifted.

She cancelled dinner and felt guilty. She finished the report at midnight and felt competent. She forgot the clothes and felt useless. The week remained normal on paper.

The paper was missing most of the work.

The Capacity Gap Map compares four things: Visible Load, Hidden Load, Available Capacity, and Recovery Access. Burnout risk grows when total load repeatedly exceeds capacity and the reader cannot obtain enough relief, support, or environmental fit to close the gap.

The map does not tell you how much you should be able to handle. It shows what your life is asking, what it costs, and what conditions are available for recovery.

Four Fields Change the Picture

Visible Load is what can be entered in a diary: paid work, caregiving, travel, housework, appointments, deadlines, study, financial problems, and practical responsibilities.

Hidden Load is the effort beneath those entries: masking, sensory filtering, uncertainty, remembering, emotional monitoring, switching, preparation, recovery, pain, and the management of other people's expectations.

Available Capacity is what you can reliably access today across thinking, movement, sensory tolerance, language, decisions, emotional range, and daily living. It is not a moral score. It changes.

Recovery Access is your real ability to obtain relief. It includes time, privacy, money, safety, control over sensory input, freedom from interruption, supportive people, and activities that restore rather than merely distract.

The Capacity Gap is not calculated with exact units. It is a decision tool. Its purpose is to reveal why two weeks containing the same visible tasks can have very different outcomes.

A week after poor sleep, conflict, illness, travel, a medication change, or several unpredictable days does not begin with the same Available Capacity as a settled week. A workday in a quiet room does not contain the same Hidden Load as the same work in an open office. Two free hours while alone are not the same as two free hours while listening for a child, expecting a delivery, and receiving work messages.

Your calendar may be accurate and still be incomplete.

Visible Load Is the Easy Part

Start with what anyone could see. Write down the demands that have consequences if they are not done.

Carmen listed paid work, school pickups, meals, laundry, the dental appointment, and dinner with her mother. That list already mattered. She had been describing herself as someone with "nothing unusual going on," even though her week contained responsibility from waking until late evening.

The danger of familiarity is that repeated load stops looking like load. A commute done every day disappears from the count. Caregiving becomes "just what I do." A recurring meeting feels less legitimate than a crisis because it is predictable, even when it drains the same amount each week.

For this map, ordinary responsibilities count.

So do wanted responsibilities. Loving your child does not make school administration free. Choosing a career does not remove the cost of meetings. Enjoying a friendship does not cancel social effort. Meaning and cost can exist together.

Action Challenge: List the Week

On one page, write every fixed or likely demand for the next seven days. Include travel, preparation, recovery, and the practical steps surrounding the main event.

Do not decide yet whether each item should stay. Visibility comes before editing.

If a task is recurring, write it anyway. Repetition does not reduce its weight.

Hidden Load Changes the Total

Hidden Load is where many AuDHD women discover why their lives feel heavier than they look.

A meeting is not one hour if you spend the morning rehearsing, the meeting monitoring your tone, and the afternoon replaying whether you interrupted. A family visit is not two hours if it requires changing clothes, tolerating an unfamiliar meal, managing touch, tracking several conversations, and recovering in silence afterward.

Masking is one form of Hidden Load. It may include forcing eye contact, controlling movement, rehearsing sentences, changing facial expression, hiding confusion, suppressing sensory distress, or copying the pace and style of other people. Qualitative and systematic research describes camouflaging as effortful and links it with exhaustion, distress, and identity related strain, while also recognizing that people may use it for safety, employment, or social access (Hull et al., 2017; Klein et al., 2025).

Switching is another form. The cost is not only doing task A and task B. It is leaving A, holding its unfinished state, entering B, learning B's rules, tolerating the change, and later trying to recover A's mental position.

Uncertainty can be load. "The engineer will arrive sometime between eight and one" may occupy five hours even if the visit takes 10 minutes. You cannot settle into a shower, leave the house, use headphones freely, or begin something you cannot interrupt.

Emotional monitoring can be load. You notice that your partner is quiet, your manager's email is shorter than usual, or your child seems worried. Even before a conversation occurs, part of your attention begins tracking the possible problem.

Hidden Load consumes capacity whether anyone praises it or not.

Available Capacity Is Today's Number

Many planning systems use a fantasy version of you. She slept well. Her medication works exactly as expected. Nobody interrupts. Her body is comfortable. The instructions are clear. She begins on time and remains the same person throughout the day.

You may meet her occasionally. She cannot be the only version allowed to make the plan.

Available Capacity changes within a day and across weeks. A noisy morning may leave speech more effortful by afternoon. A night of poor sleep may make switching harder. Hormonal changes may coincide with changes in ADHD symptoms for some women, although the evidence remains limited and varies across studies

(Osianlis et al., 2025). Pain, infection, grief, conflict, travel, and medication effects can alter access.

The aim is not to predict perfectly. It is to stop treating variation as misconduct.

Rate today's capacity in five areas:

1. Thinking and decisions
2. Sensory tolerance
3. Speech and social contact
4. Physical energy and body care
5. Starting, stopping, and switching

Use **higher**, **mixed**, or **lower**. Precise numbers may create false confidence. A simple description is enough to change a plan.

If several areas are lower, add fewer optional demands. If speech is lower but focused thinking is higher, written solo work may remain available while meetings do not. If sensory tolerance is low, the main intervention may be environmental rather than motivational.

Capacity is specific. "I have no energy" may mean "I have no social and decision capacity, but I can do a familiar repetitive task in quiet." That difference gives you choices.

Recovery Access Is Not Free Time

Zoe had three evenings without plans and still felt that she never had time to recover. She lived with two other people. The television was usually on. The kitchen light was bright. Someone spoke to her whenever she entered a shared room. Her bedroom was quiet, but work messages reached her phone and she felt responsible for answering quickly.

On paper, she had 12 free hours. In practice, she had no protected period without input, expectation, or interruption.

Recovery Access asks whether relief can actually occur.

Time is one part. Control is another.

Can you close a door? Can you lower the light? Can you decline conversation without conflict? Can you choose food without cooking? Can you stop monitoring work? Can someone else remain responsible for the children, pets, or household during the period? Can you engage with an interest without being told you are wasting time?

A person can be alone and still lack Recovery Access. Bills, unfinished tasks, pain, unsafe housing, digital contact, and fear can keep the system occupied.

A person can be with someone and recover if that person reduces demands. Quiet parallel presence may be more restorative than isolation for some readers.

Recovery Access is the condition, not the appearance.

The Four Levers

Once the map is visible, you have four places to act.

Reduce load. Remove, delay, shorten, simplify, or limit a demand.

Reveal Hidden Load. Name the sensory, social, switching, preparation, and recovery costs that have been ignored.

Add practical support. Transfer responsibility, use automation, request written instructions, prepare food differently, pay for help if possible, or ask another person to own a task.

Protect Recovery Access. Create periods with lower input, fewer decisions, clearer responsibility, and suitable stimulation.

Not every lever is equally available. Money may limit support. Employment may limit load reduction. Caregiving may limit privacy. The map should not become another way to blame yourself for conditions you did not create.

Use the lever you can reach.

Carmen could not reduce her contracted hours immediately. She could ask for the Friday report deadline to become Thursday afternoon for her contributions, which removed the Thursday night crisis. Her partner took full ownership of two school pickups rather than "helping if reminded." Carmen moved dinner with her mother to Sunday lunch, when she had more Available Capacity. She put the washing on a timer that ended when another adult was home.

None of those changes cured burnout. They closed several small parts of the gap.

Small gaps matter because they are repeated.

Build Your First Map

Draw four boxes on a page.

In **Visible Load**, write the five demands with the greatest consequences.

In **Hidden Load**, write what those demands require beneath the obvious task. Include preparation and aftermath.

In **Available Capacity**, mark what is higher, mixed, or lower this week.

In **Recovery Access**, write what relief is genuinely available and what keeps interrupting it.

Then answer three questions:

1. Which demand costs more than it appears?
2. Which form of support would remove the most repeated effort?
3. What recovery condition is missing even when time exists?

Choose one change for the next seven days.

Do not redesign your entire life from the map. A full redesign is a large project, and large projects create their own Hidden Load. The first map should lead to one change that can be tested.

Environmental Fit Comes Before Effort

A task may become easier without changing your character, motivation, or skill. The environment changes instead.

Clear written instructions reduce memory and uncertainty. Headphones reduce filtering. A predictable meeting time reduces waiting. A chair in the kitchen reduces standing. Repeated meals reduce decisions. A basket where clothes are removed reduces sorting. A text message replaces a phone call. A camera stays off. A partner takes full responsibility rather than waiting for direction.

This is not cheating. It is design.

Burnout research has emphasized the role of chronic mismatch between demands and support, while a recent systematic review identified sensory and social overwhelm, camouflaging, everyday challenges, and insufficient understanding as major contributors across studies (Raymaker et al., 2020; Ali et al., 2025).

If the environment keeps asking for unnecessary effort, trying harder may only make the mismatch less visible.

Effort is not the only variable you are allowed to change.

Principles to Remember

The Capacity Gap Map compares Visible Load, Hidden Load, Available Capacity, and Recovery Access.

Your calendar can be accurate and incomplete. It records events more easily than preparation, sensory filtering, switching, masking, and recovery.

Available Capacity changes. A useful plan accounts for the version of you who exists today, not only the version who appears on your best day.

Free time does not guarantee Recovery Access. Relief requires conditions in which pressure, responsibility, and input can actually decrease.

You have four levers: reduce load, reveal Hidden Load, add practical support, and protect Recovery Access.

The first map should create one testable change, not a new life-management project.

You do not need more discipline to solve a problem created by an incomplete count.

Chapter 3: Count the Hidden Load

Aisha's manager called her effortless.

She meant it as praise. Aisha was friendly without taking over, prepared without seeming rigid, and quick to smooth awkward moments in meetings. She remembered who had spoken, who had been interrupted, and which joke had changed the mood. New employees often sat beside her because she made the room easier to read.

Nobody saw her notes.

Before a meeting, Aisha wrote possible questions and short versions of her answers. During the meeting, she monitored her face, her hands, the volume of her voice, and how long she had been speaking. She counted two seconds before answering so she would not interrupt. When someone used an indirect phrase, she stored it for later analysis. Afterward, she replayed the meeting while writing the formal notes everyone else needed.

At home, she sometimes sat in the bathroom because it was the only room where nobody expected an expression from her.

The work that made Aisha look effortless was effort.

Hidden Load is the labor required to appear, respond, remember, adjust, and recover in ways that other people do not count. Burnout prevention becomes impossible when this load remains unnamed, because you keep planning as though only visible tasks use capacity.

Hidden Load is not proof that every ordinary expectation is unfair. It is a reason to measure the expectation honestly.

The Masking Tax

Masking can be conscious, automatic, or a mixture of both. You may suppress movement, copy another person's expression, force eye contact, hide sensory pain, rehearse conversation, soften direct language, or pretend to understand an instruction that feels unclear.

People mask for many reasons. They may want connection. They may need employment. They may have learned that visible difference brings correction, teasing, exclusion, or danger. Research on autistic camouflaging describes reasons such as social connection and protection from harm, alongside reported costs including exhaustion, identity strain, and poorer mental wellbeing (Bradley et al., 2021; Hull et al., 2017).

The **Masking Tax** is the attention and energy consumed by suppressing, rehearsing, monitoring, or replacing natural responses.

Tax is a useful word because masking may purchase something valuable. It can buy safety, privacy, smoother interaction, or access to a setting. The problem is not solved by declaring that all masking must stop. The problem is that the price is often hidden, even from the person paying it.

Aisha did not experience the process as a deliberate choice. Around other people, her face arranged itself, her voice shifted, and her attention moved toward everyone else before she noticed what she needed.

Because masking can become habitual, you may notice it only after the setting ends. Possible clues include jaw tension, headache, speech becoming harder, irritability, crying, nausea, a need for darkness, or the sense that you have disappeared from your own day.

Action Challenge: Audit One Setting

Choose one repeated setting, such as a team meeting, school pickup, family meal, appointment, or group chat. After the next occurrence, note:

1. What you controlled or monitored.
2. What you hid.
3. What you pretended to understand or tolerate.
4. What happened in your body afterward.

5. What one adjustment might lower the Masking Tax without creating unacceptable risk.

Do not begin with the hardest relationship. Begin where a small experiment is possible.

Women Are Often Praised for Carrying More

Gender expectations do not affect every woman in the same way. Culture, class, age, race, disability, sexuality, family structure, and employment all shape what is expected and what is safe to refuse.

Many late diagnosed women describe pressure to meet gendered social expectations and to mask difficulties that do not fit conventional ideas of autism or ADHD. Qualitative research with six late diagnosed AuDHD women linked adult recognition with gender norms, masking, and years of trying to explain why expected roles required unusual effort (Craddock, 2024).

The praise can make the load harder to question.

"You're so thoughtful" may mean you remember everyone's preferences.

"You're the organized one" may mean nobody else owns the calendar.

"You're good with difficult people" may mean you absorb conflict that others avoid.

"You always know what we need" may mean you are never allowed not to notice.

Competence can become a trap when it quietly transfers responsibility toward the person least able to stop monitoring.

Yvonne organized every family birthday. She bought gifts, checked addresses, reminded siblings, arranged calls, and made sure older relatives were included. She liked some parts of it. She also dreaded the six weeks around several family birthdays because the task remained mentally active every day.

When she asked her brother to take responsibility for one birthday, he said, "Just tell me what to buy."

That offer preserved the Hidden Load. Yvonne would still need to choose, remember, check, and direct. Help that requires management can reduce physical work while leaving coordination untouched.

Ownership is different. Ownership means the other person notices, decides, completes, checks, and repairs.

The distinction will return in Chapter 10 because relationship recovery often depends on transferring ownership, not assigning isolated tasks.

Switching Cost Follows You

The **Switching Cost** is the effort required to stop, start, or move between tasks, environments, people, and mental states.

A day with 10 short tasks may be harder than a day with one long task. Each transition asks your attention to release one set of rules and build another. If the previous task is unfinished, part of it may remain active while you enter the next.

Consider a morning with these visible events:

Email. Shower. Breakfast. School drop-off. Work call. Report.

The Hidden Load may include leaving an unfinished message, changing body temperature, tolerating wet skin, choosing food, finding shoes, handling traffic, shifting into a social voice, interpreting a manager's priorities, then recovering the report's mental structure after interruption.

If you plan only the minutes taken by each event, the day looks spacious. If you count the switching, it may be full.

A useful support is to group tasks by state rather than category. Make calls together. Complete outside errands in one period. Put social tasks on days with less focused work. Prepare for the next transition before the current task ends. Leave a short note stating where to restart.

This is not a rigid rule. Grouping can become boring or create an overly long block. The goal is to reduce unnecessary state changes, not build a perfect schedule.

Action Challenge: Mark the Switches

Look at tomorrow. Draw a small mark every time you will need to change location, social role, sensory setting, communication mode, or task type.

Choose one switch to remove or soften. You might move a call, prepare clothes, write the next step before stopping, eat the same breakfast, or add 10 minutes without conversation between roles.

You are not shortening only the task. You are reducing the cost of becoming the person the next task requires.

Sensory Filtering Is Work

A room does not have to be painfully loud to require constant filtering. Several conversations, a ventilation system, footsteps, screen movement, perfume, fabric, bright light, and body discomfort can create a background job that continues while you perform the visible one.

Some people notice sensory input less while they are focused on getting through a setting, then find the same light, sound, touch, or movement harder to tolerate as they become more depleted. This may look like sudden sensitivity even when the environment has not changed.

Farah worked in a shared office for six years before she began wearing headphones. She assumed the room could not be the problem because she had tolerated it for so long. Once she reduced the background speech, she noticed that she could answer messages after work. The adjustment did not make her more productive in a dramatic way. It returned part of her evening.

That outcome matters.

An adjustment should not be judged only by how much more work it extracts. It can be valuable because it leaves enough capacity for food, conversation, or sleep.

Sensory support may include changing light, clothes, sound, temperature, smell, posture, movement, visual clutter, or the timing of exposure. The most useful change is often ordinary and specific.

"Reduce sensory overload" is too broad to act on.

"Use the smaller meeting room without the projector fan" is a plan.

Emotional Monitoring Uses Attention

Emotional monitoring is the work of tracking how everyone else is doing and what their state might require from you.

It can look like empathy. It can also become vigilance.

You notice the sigh, the short reply, the cupboard door, the silence, the changed punctuation, or the look exchanged across a room. Your mind begins producing possible causes and responses. Should you ask? Wait? Reassure? Apologize? Change the plan? Perform normality?

This process may continue even when nobody has asked you to take responsibility.

Some readers developed it in unpredictable homes. Some learned it through repeated social misunderstanding. Some were rewarded for being helpful. Some use detailed observation as a way to compensate for social information that is not automatically clear.

Whatever the origin, monitoring has a cost.

One practical boundary is to separate noticing from ownership.

You can notice that another person is quiet. That does not automatically create a task.

You can ask once whether something needs discussion. You do not have to build 12 explanations in silence.

You can let an adult name what they need rather than continuously adjusting to clues.

This may feel unsafe at first. Begin in relationships where direct communication is possible.

Build the Hidden Load List

Write down one ordinary day. Under each visible activity, add the hidden work in five categories:

1. Preparation
2. Sensory filtering
3. Masking or social monitoring
4. Switching and interruption
5. Recovery afterward

Then circle anything another person, a tool, or an environmental change could reduce.

Do not use the list to prove that your life is impossible. Use it to find repeated effort that does not have to remain yours.

A repeated two minute decision can matter more than a rare two hour task. A daily conversation in an uncomfortable room can matter more than a monthly event. Burnout is often built through accumulation.

The load you repeat deserves priority.

What Readers Are Tired of Hearing

"Everyone gets tired."

"You're overthinking."

"You need better boundaries."

"Just ask for help."

Each sentence may contain a small truth and still fail because it ignores the mechanism.

Everyone gets tired. Not everyone loses reliable access to speech, food preparation, sensory tolerance, and ordinary tasks after maintaining a socially acceptable day.

You may be thinking in detail because the setting requires manual processing.

A boundary is not useful until it names the specific demand, person, and consequence.

Help is not helpful when you must identify, assign, explain, remind, and check every step.

Specificity turns a vague recommendation into a reduction in Hidden Load.

Your Hidden Load Audit

Hidden Load includes masking, sensory filtering, switching, uncertainty, emotional monitoring, preparation, and recovery.

The Masking Tax may purchase safety or access. Its cost still needs to be counted.

Praise can conceal responsibility. Being capable does not mean you should remain the owner of every repeated task.

Help reduces load only when it does not require you to keep managing the helper.

Switching can make a day full even when each visible task is short.

An adjustment can be successful because it returns your evening, not only because it increases output.

You cannot protect capacity from a cost you have been trained not to count.

Chapter 4: Look Beyond One Explanation

Similar symptoms need context before they need certainty.

A good explanation should organize your experience without closing the door on other causes. AuDHD burnout can coexist with depression, sleep problems, medication effects, pain, hormonal change, nutritional deficiency, chronic illness, and ordinary life stress.

This chapter will not teach you to diagnose yourself. It will help you notice when a pattern deserves broader assessment and prepare information that makes a professional conversation more useful.

Similar Symptoms Need Context

Grace had spent six months calling everything burnout.

The exhaustion made sense. Work had become louder and less predictable after an office move. She was masking more, sleeping badly, and using every weekend to recover. Her tolerance for food textures had narrowed. She cried after ordinary interruptions. The AuDHD burnout description fitted so well that she stopped asking whether anything else might also be happening.

Then she became breathless on the stairs.

She explained that away too. Burnout made everything harder. She bought more ready meals, cancelled plans, and waited for rest to work. When a friend persuaded her to make a medical appointment, blood tests identified iron deficiency anemia.

Treatment did not remove the sensory strain at work. It did not make meetings easy or restore every lost routine. It did return part of her physical energy. The burnout framework had been useful. It had also become too complete.

Fatigue is one of the least specific symptoms a person can have. It can appear with insufficient sleep, stress, depression, infection, anemia, thyroid conditions, chronic pain, medication effects, hormonal change, sleep disorders, and many other conditions. The

NHS advises seeking medical advice when unexplained tiredness has lasted for several weeks, affects daily life, or occurs with other concerning changes (National Health Service, 2023c).

Concentration problems are also nonspecific. So are withdrawal, irritability, reduced appetite, changes in sleep, and difficulty beginning tasks.

The pattern around a symptom can provide useful information:

When did it begin?

Did it follow a change in work, health, medication, sleep, relationship stress, infection, pregnancy, or hormones?

Does it improve in lower demand and lower sensory settings?

Does it appear with low mood or loss of interest across nearly everything?

Does physical or mental activity produce a delayed worsening that feels medically different from ordinary tiredness?

Are there new physical signs, such as breathlessness, fainting, persistent pain, weakness, weight change, fever, or unusual bleeding?

You are not expected to interpret every answer. The timeline helps a clinician see what changed and what should be considered.

Burnout and Depression Can Overlap

Autistic burnout research describes exhaustion, reduced function, withdrawal, and increased sensitivity. Depression can involve low mood, reduced interest or pleasure, sleep and appetite changes, hopelessness, poor concentration, and reduced functioning. The overlap is real. Measurement research has found associations between autistic burnout and depression, and early tools have not always separated them cleanly (Arnold et al., 2023).

The distinction cannot be reduced to one sentence such as "burnout improves with rest while depression does not." Real lives are not that tidy. A person can feel some relief in a quiet setting and still be depressed. A person can remain interested in one narrow activity while experiencing severe depression. Burnout may coexist with grief or hopelessness. Depression can also affect concentration, motivation, sleep, appetite, and daily functioning, which can make the overall picture harder to interpret.

Ask for help when low mood persists, coping is becoming harder, or attempts to improve the situation are not helping. The NHS advises speaking with a clinician when low mood lasts more than two weeks, is difficult to manage, or is affecting daily life (National Health Service, 2022).

If you are thinking about harming yourself, feel unable to remain safe, or are in immediate danger, seek urgent local help now. Do not wait for a clearer label.

A useful professional can consider more than one explanation at once.

Burnout and Physical Illness Can Coexist

Nadia developed severe fatigue after a viral illness. She also had a demanding job and a recent autism diagnosis. Everyone around her, including Nadia, assumed the crash was psychological and neurodivergent.

She noticed one difference. Activity did not only tire her. It sometimes produced a delayed worsening with flu-like feelings, body pain, and much poorer thinking the next day. That pattern required medical discussion, not a more disciplined recovery schedule.

Myalgic encephalomyelitis or chronic fatigue syndrome, often written as ME/CFS, is one example of a condition that may involve severe fatigue, unrefreshing sleep, cognitive problems, and worsening after activity. It is not the same as autistic burnout, and this book does not provide a way to diagnose it. NHS guidance recommends medical assessment and exclusion of other causes when this pattern is suspected (National Health Service, 2024a).

The point is not to make you afraid of every symptom. It is to protect you from assuming that neurodivergence explains any physical change.

New and persistent symptoms deserve their own attention.

Medication Deserves a Real Review

Medication can affect sleep, appetite, heart rate, mood, and concentration. Benefits and unwanted effects may also vary across the day or as health and routines change (National Institute for Health and Care Excellence, 2018).

Do not change prescribed medication solely because a book or online post says it should help or harm burnout. Speak with the prescriber or another appropriately qualified professional.

A useful medication review includes more than "Is it working?" NICE guidance for adult ADHD recommends ongoing review of benefits, adverse effects, clinical need, and the person's preferences. It also places environmental modifications alongside medication rather than treating medication as the only response to impairment (National Institute for Health and Care Excellence, 2018).

Before an appointment, write:

1. The medication and dose you take.
2. When you take it.
3. What becomes easier.
4. What becomes harder.
5. What happens as it wears off.
6. Changes in sleep, appetite, anxiety, heart symptoms, or mood.
7. Any pattern across the menstrual cycle, pregnancy, postpartum period, or perimenopause.

The prescriber needs a pattern, not a perfect explanation.

Create a Symptom Timeline

A symptom timeline is one of the most useful low effort tools in this book. It prevents the appointment from becoming a test of memory under pressure.

Use one page. Across the top, write the last six to 12 months. Down the side, write these categories:

Physical energy
Sleep
Mood and interest
Sensory tolerance
Thinking and memory
Speech and communication
Food and appetite
Medication
Menstrual or hormonal changes, if relevant
Major demands or life events

Mark when each area changed. Approximate dates are enough.

Then add three sentences:

"My main concern is __________."
"This is affecting daily life by __________."
"I would like help considering __________."

The third blank can include burnout, depression, sleep, medication effects, blood tests, hormones, pain, or another concern. You are not ordering a diagnosis. You are making the full question visible.

Action Challenge: Prepare the Appointment Page

Bring the timeline, medication list, and three sentences to the appointment. If speech becomes difficult, hand over the page or send it in advance where possible.

You can also bring a person who understands the practical changes. Choose someone who will add information rather than speak over you.

When Professionals Minimize the Pattern

Some women reach an appointment after years of appearing composed. They explain severe difficulty in a calm voice, and the calmness is mistaken for mild symptoms.

You may need to describe function rather than emotion.

Instead of "I am very tired," say, "I am eating crackers for dinner four nights a week because I cannot sequence cooking after work."

Instead of "Noise is worse," say, "I now leave meetings to sit in the toilet because ordinary office sound becomes painful."

Instead of "I am struggling," say, "I missed two medication doses and three bill payments this month, which is new for me."

Specific examples show consequence.

If a concern is dismissed, you can ask:

"What alternatives have been considered?"

"What signs would mean I should return?"

"Can you record that this is affecting my daily functioning?"

"What is the next step if this does not improve?"

You may also seek another opinion where your health system and circumstances allow.

Being calm is not evidence that the problem is small.

Urgent Changes Need Urgent Help

A self-help book should not become a waiting room when immediate care is needed.

Seek urgent local help if you are in danger, cannot keep yourself safe, have severe or rapidly worsening symptoms, or experience sudden confusion, severe difficulty breathing, chest tightness or heaviness, or another acute medical concern. NHS guidance treats sudden confusion and severe breathing difficulty as emergencies.

Outside the UK, use the equivalent local emergency or crisis service (National Health Service, 2024b, 2024c).

If you are caring for children or another dependent person and your functioning has fallen below what is needed for safety, ask for immediate practical support. This is not a moral verdict. It is a response to capacity.

A crisis is not the time to prove independence.

Hold More Than One Cause

After treatment for anemia, Grace still needed changes at work. The lights remained harsh. The new office remained noisy. Her meetings remained stacked without recovery time. She was physically better and still burnt out.

This was not evidence that the medical treatment had failed. It meant two problems had been present.

Your map may also contain several layers. Sleep deprivation can lower Available Capacity. Masking can increase Hidden Load. Depression can reduce access to interest and action. Pain can consume attention. Hormonal change can alter symptoms. A job can remain badly fitted.

The most useful plan may include medical care, mental health support, environmental change, practical help, and reduced demands.

One explanation is comforting because it feels simple. A wider explanation is often more useful because it gives you more than one place to act.

When Memory Fails in Appointments

Appointments often require the functions that burnout has reduced. You must remember a long pattern, choose the most important details, speak in order, interpret questions, and remain socially composed in an unfamiliar setting. Leaving without saying the main concern does not mean the concern was minor.

Prepare for reduced access rather than hoping it will disappear in the room.

Put the main issue at the top of the page. Use dates where you know them and approximations where you do not. Bring photographs of medication labels, screenshots of trackers, or a short written account from someone who sees the daily changes. Ask the clinician to summarize the plan in writing.

If a question is too broad, ask for a narrower version. “Tell me about the fatigue” can become “When did it begin?” followed by “What makes it worse?” You are allowed to take time before answering.

At the end, repeat the next step:

“You are ordering these tests.”

“I should continue the medication as prescribed.”

“I should return in four weeks or sooner if these signs appear.”

This repetition is not unnecessary. It protects the plan after the appointment ends.

Avoid the Single Checklist Trap

Online checklists can create recognition, but they rarely establish cause. A list of autistic burnout signs may overlap with depression, sleep disorders, chronic illness, medication effects, and severe stress. A hormone checklist may overlap with thyroid problems, anemia, pregnancy, or medication changes.

Use checklists to collect questions, not settle them.

A helpful next step sounds like, “These eight changes appeared over three months and affect eating, work, and sleep. I want to consider burnout and rule out other causes.”

A less safe conclusion sounds like, “The checklist proves this is burnout, so no medical review is needed.”

The first keeps the framework useful. The second makes it a barrier.

Principles to Remember

AuDHD burnout can be a useful framework without being the only explanation.

Fatigue, poor concentration, withdrawal, sleep changes, and reduced function occur in many physical and mental health conditions.

Burnout and depression can coexist. New or persistent low mood, loss of interest, hopelessness, or difficulty coping deserve support.

New, severe, rapidly worsening, or medically unusual symptoms deserve assessment.

Medication changes belong in a professional review. Record benefits, adverse effects, timing, and patterns rather than changing treatment from online advice.

Describe function. “I cannot prepare food after work” gives a clinician more information than “I feel bad.”

A useful explanation opens routes to help. It does not close the case.

Chapter 5: Stop Digging

Samira had a new recovery plan every Monday.

One week, she decided to wake earlier, walk before work, cook protein-rich meals, meditate, answer messages at lunch, and go to bed without her phone. The next week, she bought a planner and divided every day into blocks. Then she created a cleaning schedule because the clutter was making her feel worse.

Each plan made sense on its own. Together, they added more decisions, more transitions, more tracking, and more evidence that she was failing.

On Thursday night, Samira stood in the kitchen surrounded by vegetables she no longer had the energy to prepare. She ordered food, felt guilty about the money, and stayed awake late trying to redesign the plan.

She did not need a better system for doing more. She needed to stop adding demands to a life that already exceeded capacity.

The first stage of recovery is not improvement. It is stabilization. You reduce immediate damage, protect basic needs, and stop treating every problem as a project that must be solved this week.

This is where the Capacity Gap Map becomes practical. You are not required to close every gap. You are trying to stop widening it.

Recovery Can Become Another Performance

Burnout advice often arrives as a collection of worthy activities: regular exercise, nutritious food, sleep hygiene, therapy, journaling, sunlight, social connection, relaxation, hydration, boundaries, and a tidy environment.

Each may help in the right form and at the right time. During severe depletion, the combined list can become impossible.

A person with low Available Capacity may hear "take care of your health" as 14 new tasks. She now has to research meals, shop, cook, wash up, choose exercise, schedule appointments, monitor sleep, track water, and feel guilty about all of it.

Stabilization asks a different question:

What must remain safe enough this week?

The answer may be less attractive than an ideal routine. It may include ready meals, paper plates, cancelled plans, repeated clothes, delayed cleaning, automatic replies, and asking someone else to make decisions.

Temporary simplification is not your new identity. It is an intervention.

Sort by Consequence

Take every active demand and place it in one of four groups.

Essential means there is a serious near term consequence for health, safety, housing, income, dependents, or legal responsibilities.

Delayable means it matters but can move without serious immediate harm.

Delegable means another person, service, tool, or simplified system could own it.

Removable means the task exists because of habit, appearance, guilt, or an outdated expectation and can be stopped.

Be strict about the word essential. A work task may be essential. Doing it to your usual standard may not be. Eating is essential. Cooking from scratch is not. Medication may be essential. Organizing the entire cupboard is not.

Maya used this method during a severe crash. Her essential list contained medication, feeding herself, caring for her cat, one work deadline, and paying rent. She delayed a nonurgent dental cleaning, delegated grocery shopping, and removed two social commitments and a volunteer task.

The list did not make her feel instantly better. It stopped the week from creating five new crises.

Action Challenge: Make the Four Groups

Use one page. Write no more than seven items in each group. If the essential group contains 20 items, several are probably standards, methods, or preferences rather than the essential outcome.

Choose one delay, one transfer, and one removal today.

The goal is not bravery. It is less load by tonight.

Build a Minimum Viable Day

The **Minimum Viable Day** is the smallest safe version of a day during severe burnout.

It is not a failed normal day. It is a separate operating plan.

Your version may include:

1. Take essential medication.
2. Drink and eat enough to remain safe.
3. Meet one unavoidable responsibility.
4. Complete basic care for a dependent person or animal.
5. Reduce sensory and social input.

That may be the whole day.

A Minimum Viable Day should not contain improvement goals. It should not include "catch up," "sort life out," or "exercise unless exhausted." If movement helps, it can be offered as an option, not a condition for success.

Write acceptable low effort versions beside each item. Food may be cereal, a sandwich, a meal replacement prescribed or suitable for you, or delivery. During a severe low-capacity period, a temporary hygiene minimum may include wipes, clean underwear, mouth care, or sitting in the shower. These options reduce immediate barriers. They are not equivalent to full dental or medical care when a health problem is present. Communication may be one sentence sent to several people.

The smallest safe version counts.

Reduce Decisions Before Tasks

Decisions are often the hidden part of a task.

"Eat dinner" may require choosing what, checking ingredients, comparing effort, predicting sensory tolerance, deciding whether to spend money, and estimating how much cleanup will follow.

Reducing the task without reducing decisions may not help. A full fridge can be harder than three predictable options.

Create defaults for low capacity periods:

A short list of acceptable foods.

A repeated outfit.

A standard message for cancellations.

A fixed location for medication and keys.

A default delivery order.

A rule for which calls go unanswered.

Defaults are not forever. They protect thinking access while it is strained.

Samira chose three dinners for the week and gave her partner full authority to select among them. She stopped reopening the decision at five o'clock. The change saved more capacity than the expensive planner had.

A decision you do not have to remake is a form of support.

Use Three Recovery Routes

Not everyone can take extended leave. Recovery advice should say this plainly.

This book uses three broad planning routes. They are not clinical stages, and you may move between them.

Emergency reduction applies when functioning has fallen sharply or safety is at risk. It may include sick leave, urgent medical care, family support, pausing study, or temporary relief from caregiving.

Partial reduction applies when some responsibilities can change. It may include fewer hours, remote work, cancelled social plans, simplified meals, reduced household standards, or staged return.

Working through harm reduction applies when income or responsibility makes major leave impossible. The aim is not full recovery while the main load remains unchanged. The aim is to prevent further damage by reducing every avoidable cost around the fixed demand.

Working through may mean wearing the same comfortable clothes, using transport that reduces sensory strain, declining optional meetings, eating repetitive food, stopping all nonessential volunteering, and going directly into protected recovery after work.

It may feel unfair that so much of life has to shrink around employment. The map is allowed to reveal unfairness. It still needs to help you survive the current week.

Ask for Practical Help

A vague offer such as "Reach out if you need something" creates another task. You must identify the need, decide whether it is acceptable, formulate the request, and tolerate the uncertainty of the response.

Specific offers are easier:

"I can bring two meals on Tuesday. Would that help?"

"I can take full responsibility for the school pickup this week."

"I can sit with you while you call the doctor, or I can write the message for you."

When you ask, use the same level of detail.

"I need help" may be true but difficult to act on.

"Please order groceries from this saved list and put them away without asking me to approve substitutions" transfers a complete task.

If another adult shares the household, ask for ownership rather than assistance. Ownership includes noticing, planning, remembering, completing, and fixing.

Action Challenge: Transfer One Whole Task

Choose one repeated task. Write down every part of it. Ask one person to take the whole sequence for a defined period.

If nobody is available, look for a tool or simplification that removes at least two steps. Automation, delivery, duplicates, timers, and visible storage can count.

Support is measured by effort removed.

Lower the Standard on Purpose

Lowering standards can feel dangerous for women whose competence has protected them from criticism.

You may worry that one ready meal will become permanent, one cancelled plan will damage a friendship, or one messy room will prove what other people already suspect.

The fear is understandable. It also keeps the high standard in place when the body can no longer fund it.

Choose a temporary standard and name the end point.

“For two weeks, clean clothes can stay in baskets.”

“Until the work deadline passes, dinner will come from five low effort options.”

“For the rest of this month, I will not host.”

“During the current crash, replies may take seven days.”

A temporary rule reduces daily negotiation.

You are not lowering every standard. You are choosing which standard will stop consuming capacity while something more important is protected.

Do Not Spend the First Good Day

A good morning after several bad days can feel like release. You notice the dishes, messages, paperwork, exercise, shopping, and unfinished plans. Relief becomes urgency. By evening, the available energy is gone. The next day looks like failure again.

Treat the first improvement as evidence to observe, not a debt collection opportunity.

Use only part of the apparent extra capacity. Protect the rest. Add one task, not eight. Check the delayed cost before adding more.

This practice may feel painfully slow. It is still faster than repeating a complete crash.

The first good day belongs partly to tomorrow.

Your Seven Day Stabilization Plan

Write no more than five daily essentials. Add one recovery condition and one support request.

Example:

Daily essentials: medication, two meals and snacks, water, feed the cat, attend one required work block.

Recovery condition: no conversation for 30 minutes after work.

Support request: partner owns dinner and cleanup for seven days.

Anything else is optional.

At the end of the week, ask:

Did safety improve?

Did fewer new problems appear?

Which demand remained most damaging?

What support removed real effort?

Stabilization is successful when the rate of harm slows, even if you do not yet feel recovered.

Stabilize When You Live Alone

Living alone can provide sensory control and remove social demands. It can also mean that nobody sees the decline, brings food, notices missed medication, or takes over when a task fails.

Create support that does not depend on a crisis conversation. Choose one person who can receive a short status message. Agree on what silence means and when they should check again. Keep essential contacts in one place. Arrange deliveries before supplies are gone. Use visible medication and food systems where safe.

A simple private check can use three words:

"Green" means no action is currently needed.

"Amber" means a practical check tomorrow.

"Red" means call, visit if agreed, or help contact the appropriate service.

This is a communication shorthand, not a clinical triage scale.

Do not give someone emergency responsibility without asking whether they can hold it. A real plan includes consent, limits, and another route if they are unavailable.

Externalize the Next Step

During burnout, remembering that a task exists may not produce access to the first action. Leave the next step outside your mind.

Instead of a note saying "sort bills," write "open the brown envelope and put the due date in the calendar." Instead of "clean kitchen," write "put food rubbish in one bag." Instead of "contact work," prepare the message and recipient before the day it may be needed.

The next step should be small enough to begin without another planning session.

This is scaffolding, not a promise that you will finish. A visible first step shortens the distance between noticing and action.

Principles to Remember

The first stage of recovery is stabilization, not optimization.

Useful health advice can become harmful when it arrives as 14 new demands.

Sort tasks into essential, delayable, delegable, and removable. Protect outcomes, not preferred methods.

A Minimum Viable Day is a separate plan for severe periods. It is not a failed version of normal life.

Reduce decisions as well as tasks. Defaults protect thinking access.

If full leave is impossible, reduce every avoidable cost around the fixed demand.

The first good day is not permission to collect every postponed task.

Stop making recovery compete with the life that caused the crash.

Chapter 6: Build Rest That Works

Priya had spent the whole Saturday resting.

She stayed in bed until late, watched familiar television, scrolled through short videos, ordered food, and declined a friend's invitation. By evening, her body was still heavy and her thoughts felt louder. She was bored, guilty, overstimulated, and no more able to prepare for Monday.

The day looked restful because it contained little visible activity. It did not contain much relief.

Her phone supplied constant movement. Messages remained unanswered. Work sat open on a laptop beside the bed. The television and videos competed for attention. Each time Priya became bored, she searched for something more stimulating, then felt worse from the speed and noise.

She had stopped moving. The demands had not stopped reaching her.

Rest works when it changes the kind or amount of pressure reaching you and leaves some part of you more available afterward. For some people, rest may work better when it combines reduced demand with enough gentle interest to prevent boredom or agitation from adding more strain.

The goal is not to find the perfect restful activity. It is to build options for different states.

Sleep and Recovery Differ

Sleep is essential. It is not the only form of recovery.

You can sleep for many hours and wake unrefreshed because sleep quality is poor, illness is present, medication is affecting sleep, pain is active, or the total load remains too high. Persistent unexplained fatigue or unrefreshing sleep deserves medical discussion rather than endless attempts to improve a bedtime routine alone (National Health Service, 2023c).

Recovery also occurs while awake. Sensory pressure can fall. Decisions can stop. Social performance can end. The mind can engage with a familiar interest. The body can move in a way that feels regulating. Responsibility can be transferred.

A useful question is: what needs a break?

If the main problem is sensory overload, conversation may not be rest even if you love the person.

If the main problem is boredom and mental agitation, lying in silence may not help.

If the main problem is decision fatigue, an open day with no plan may create more work.

If the main problem is masking, being with someone who expects performance may keep the same cost active.

Rest should answer the actual load.

Build a Rest Menu

A Rest Menu is a prepared list of options divided by Available Capacity. You create it before choosing becomes difficult.

Zero energy options require almost no setup. Examples may include darkness, ear protection, a familiar audio track, lying under a weighted or preferred blanket if safe and comfortable, a preselected program, a simple repetitive phone game, or quiet parallel presence.

Low energy options require a small amount of action. They may include a shower with altered lighting, sitting outside, a familiar craft, gentle stretching, an audiobook, sorting a collection, or a slow walk in a known place.

Moderate energy options may include time with a trusted person, cooking something familiar, a longer walk, gaming with friends, gardening, swimming, or focused time on an interest.

The examples are not instructions. Some will be irritating, inaccessible, expensive, physically unsuitable, or unpleasant for you.

Choose activities that answer these questions:

Does this lower demand?

Does it reduce or improve sensory input?
Does it contain enough interest?
Can I stop without a difficult transition?
How do I usually feel afterward?

Action Challenge: Make Three Columns

Write three headings: zero, low, and moderate. Add three options to each. Keep the list visible.

If you cannot think of nine, begin with three total. The menu should reduce decisions, not become a creativity test.

Sensory Reduction and Sensory Nourishment

Rest is often described as removing stimulation. Some people also recover through chosen stimulation.

Uncontrolled sound can exhaust you while a repeated song helps. Bright overhead light can hurt while sunlight through a curtain feels good. Crowded movement can overwhelm you while rocking, pacing, stretching, or swimming settles the body.

The difference may involve predictability, control, intensity, meaning, and the ability to stop.

Sensory reduction lowers input. Sensory nourishment provides input you choose.

Dalia spent years trying to recover in a silent bedroom because silence sounded like the correct answer to overload. After 20 minutes, her thoughts accelerated and she reached for her phone. She later discovered that a familiar instrumental playlist and a slow puzzle gave her mind enough structure to settle.

The room did not become more stimulating in every way. It became more suitable.

Ask what your system is seeking, not only what it is avoiding.

Interest Is Not a Reward

ADHD advice often treats interest as a prize given after the important work. For some AuDHD people, interest is also a source of regulation, attention, and restoration.

Research with autistic adults has found positive associations between special interests and several areas of subjective wellbeing, while also suggesting that extremely intense engagement can have costs when it crowds out other needs (Grove et al., 2018).

A valued interest can provide familiarity, competence, pleasure, structure, and relief from social interpretation. It may be one of the few places where attention does not have to be forced.

That does not mean every long period of focus is restorative. Check the aftermath.

Did you eat, drink, and use the bathroom?

Could you stop without distress?

Did the activity reduce mental noise or intensify it?

Did it support sleep or displace it?

Did you feel more like yourself or less aware of your body until a crash?

Interest is allowed to be part of recovery. It also needs conditions that protect essential care.

Scrolling Can Help and Harm

Scrolling is easy to moralize. It can provide novelty, distraction, social contact, and immediate access during low capacity. It can also deliver rapid sound, movement, comparison, distressing information, advertising, and endless switching.

The useful question is not whether scrolling is good. It is what kind, for how long, and with what result.

Try a simple experiment. Before opening an app, name the need:

"I need novelty."

"I need company without conversation."

"I need to avoid thinking for 10 minutes."

"I am too tired to choose anything else."

Set a gentle stopping cue if that helps, such as one episode, one saved playlist, a phone timer, or moving the charger away from the bed. Then check whether you are more settled, more activated, or unchanged.

If scrolling is the only accessible relief, do not remove it without replacing the function it serves.

Demand Free Time Has Rules

Time is not demand free simply because nobody scheduled an event.

A real demand free period may require agreements:

Nobody asks you to decide dinner.

Work notifications are off.

You are not the person listening for children.

You do not have to respond to messages.

The house may remain untidy.

You can leave an activity without explanation.

Grace and her partner used the phrase "off duty" for a 45 minute period after work. During that time, Grace did not answer household questions unless something was urgent. Her partner owned the meal decision and any child requests. The boundary worked because responsibility changed, not because Grace sat alone while still listening for her name.

Rest requires release from responsibility, not only permission to sit down.

Action Challenge: Protect One Recovery Condition

Choose one 20 to 60 minute period this week. Protect one condition that is usually missing: no decisions, no speech, lower light, no work contact, no caregiving responsibility, chosen sound, or uninterrupted interest.

Keep the experiment small enough to defend.

Afterward, record one change in speech, food, movement, sensory tolerance, or thinking. "No change" is useful data.

Movement Is Optional and Specific

Movement helps some people settle, sleep, think, or discharge agitation. It makes others feel worse when pain, illness, severe depletion, or post-exertional symptoms are present.

"Exercise more" is too broad to be safe or useful.

Movement can mean standing outside for two minutes, stretching in bed, rocking, walking around the room, dancing to one song, or following a medical rehabilitation plan. It can also mean no added movement today.

If activity repeatedly causes a delayed and medically concerning worsening, seek professional advice rather than forcing progression.

Rest should not become a fitness test.

Quiet Company Can Count

Some readers recover best alone. Others become more dysregulated in isolation.

Quiet company, sometimes called parallel presence, allows two people to share space without continuous interaction. One person reads while the other plays a game. A friend sits nearby while you sort food or make a phone call. A partner watches television without expecting conversation.

The company can reduce loneliness and initiation demands. It can also become social work if you feel responsible for entertaining, reassuring, or monitoring the other person.

Choose people who can tolerate your reduced availability.

A supportive person does not turn your silence into an emergency they need you to solve.

Measure Restoration by Access

Rest may not produce a feeling of energy. During severe burnout, the result may be smaller.

You can tolerate the kitchen light long enough to eat.

You can answer one necessary message.

Your jaw releases.

You can choose between two foods.

Speech becomes slightly easier.

You stop replaying the meeting.

You can sleep.

These are signs of increased access.

Use a simple before and after check. Rate speech, decisions, sensory tolerance, body tension, and ability to complete one basic task as lower, unchanged, or higher.

Over time, your Rest Menu becomes based on evidence from your own life rather than generic advice.

The best rest is not the activity that looks healthiest. It is the one that reduces the load you are actually carrying without creating a larger cost afterward.

The Transition Into Rest Matters

You may reach free time while still carrying the speed of the previous task. Your body is home, but your attention is in the meeting, traffic, school pickup, or conversation. Asking yourself to relax immediately can feel impossible.

Use a short transition that stays the same. Change clothes. Wash your hands. Eat something predictable. Lower one light. Write the unfinished thought on paper. Play one familiar track. Sit in the same chair.

The sequence tells your system that one state has ended. It also removes the decision about how to begin resting.

Keep the transition short. A 12 step evening ritual can become another standard to fail.

When Rest Creates More Agitation

Some people become more aware of distress when activity stops. The quiet makes unfinished thoughts louder. Body sensations become clearer. Guilt arrives. You may stand up repeatedly, begin small tasks, or search for intense stimulation.

Do not interpret agitation as proof that rest is impossible. Change the form.

Use bounded activity. Fold the same towels. Walk a familiar route. Listen to a known audiobook while lying down. Sort objects connected with an interest. Sit with someone who does not require conversation.

The activity gives attention a rail to run on while other demands decrease.

If quiet repeatedly brings panic, intrusive thoughts, severe low mood, or memories that feel unmanageable, professional support may be appropriate. The Rest Menu is not a treatment for every source of distress.

Stop Before the Rest Activity Turns

An activity may begin as restoration and become another drain. A game extends past sleep. Research on an interest becomes 30 open tabs. A short conversation becomes emotional support for someone else.

Choose a stopping cue before you begin. The cue might be an episode ending, a timer, a meal, the end of a playlist, or another person leaving. A cue is not a command to stop regardless of how you feel. It gives you a moment to decide again.

Rest remains restorative partly because you can leave it.

Check Whether the Rest Worked

Rest works when it changes the pressure reaching you and returns some access.

Sleep is essential, but persistent unexplained fatigue or unrefreshing sleep deserves assessment.

For some people, rest may need both reduced demand and enough chosen interest to prevent boredom or agitation from adding strain.

Sensory reduction and sensory nourishment are different. Both can support recovery.

Interests are not merely rewards. They can provide familiarity, regulation, competence, and pleasure.

Do not remove an accessible coping activity until you understand the function it serves.

Demand free time requires a transfer of responsibility, not only an empty calendar.

Rest is measured by what becomes more available afterward.

Chapter 7: Protect the Basics

Elena stood outside the shower for 20 minutes.

She wanted to get in. She had a medical appointment later and knew clean hair would make her feel less exposed. The towel was ready. The water was warm. Nothing was technically preventing her.

The task still contained too many changes.

Clothes off. Cold air. Water sound. Temperature adjustment. Wet hair against skin. Soap smell. Standing. Turning the water off. Cold again. Drying. Choosing clothes. Managing damp hair. Leaving the quiet bathroom for the appointment.

When Elena finally walked away without showering, she felt ashamed of failing at a basic task.

The task was basic only in the sense that people do it routinely. It was not simple.

When burnout reduces access, protect the outcome by creating smaller, supported, and more tolerable versions of essential tasks. Food, hygiene, medication, home, and money do not need ideal routines. They need safe enough systems that still work when capacity is low.

The goal of this chapter is not to make you independent at all costs. It is to reduce the number of steps between you and basic care.

Break the Task at the Barrier

A broad instruction such as "take a shower" hides the point where access fails.

For Elena, the strongest barriers were temperature changes, wet hair, standing, and the transition into the appointment. Telling her to use a checklist would not reduce those sensory and physical costs.

She created three versions of hygiene.

The minimum version used wipes, deodorant, clean underwear, and teeth cleaned in the easiest available form.

The supported version meant sitting in the shower, keeping hair dry, using the same unscented products, and warming the room first.

The standard version was a full shower and hair wash on a day without an immediate transition afterward.

The minimum version reduced immediate barriers and protected some comfort. It was a temporary fallback, not a claim that every reduced option is equivalent to full care. The supported version became easier to reach. The standard version stopped being the only version that counted.

Use the same approach for any daily task.

What is the required outcome?

Where does access fail?

What can be removed, changed, prepared, or transferred?

A smaller version should preserve the outcome that matters most. It does not have to resemble the usual method.

Food Must Be Available Before Hunger

When you have not eaten, thinking and emotional control may become harder for some people. Burnout can also make the steps required to obtain food less available. The result is a loop. You need food to function, but reduced functioning makes food harder to access.

"Meal planning" can be too large. Begin with a food ladder.

Immediate foods can be eaten without preparation. Examples include fruit, cheese, yogurt, crackers, cereal bars, nuts if safe for you, ready drinks, or foods already portioned.

Assembly foods require one or two steps. Examples include cereal, sandwiches, microwave rice with a protein, soup, frozen meals, toast, or snack plates.

Prepared foods require more capacity but can create leftovers. These can be familiar meals with predictable ingredients and low cleanup.

Choose foods that are accessible to you. Sensory restrictions, allergies, medical needs, culture, cost, and eating disorders all matter. This book cannot prescribe a diet.

Lin kept a box beside the sofa containing shelf stable foods and drinks. She had resisted the idea because eating there felt untidy. During burnout, the box prevented long periods without food when walking to the kitchen and choosing became inaccessible.

A support is allowed to look unusual if it works.

Action Challenge: Build One Food Station

Choose one place where you repeatedly become stuck. Put enough acceptable food and drink there for one low capacity period. Include anything needed to open or eat it.

If food availability is unreliable because of money, housing, caregiving, or access, seek local practical support. Food banks, community services, benefits advice, family help, and health professionals may be part of the plan. The problem is not solved by a better container.

Medication Needs Fewer Failure Points

Medication routines can fail through forgetting, losing track of time, uncertainty about whether a dose was taken, difficulty obtaining refills, or avoiding the sensory experience of swallowing.

Reduce failure points where medically appropriate.

Keep medication in a visible but safe location.

Use a dated organizer if suitable.

Pair the dose with one reliable event rather than an ambitious morning routine.

Set refill reminders well before medication runs out.

Ask a pharmacy about delivery or automatic refill options where available.

Use a written record if double dosing is a risk.

Do not crush tablets, open capsules, alter how a medicine is taken, change its timing, or combine it with food without checking the label and asking a pharmacist or prescriber. Some formulations can stop working properly or become unsafe when altered (National Health Service, 2023b). "Make it easier" still has to remain medically safe.

If medication management has become unreliable, tell the prescriber, pharmacist, or a trusted person. This is practical information, not evidence that you cannot be trusted.

The Home Can Hold the Instructions

Many household systems depend on memory. Objects are stored where they look tidy rather than where they are used. Supplies are kept in one central place, which creates extra movement and remembering. Laundry must pass through several stages before it counts as done.

A burnout friendly home holds more of the sequence for you.

Put duplicates where the task occurs. Keep cleaning wipes in the bathroom. Put a rubbish bin beside the place where packaging collects. Store medication beside the event connected with taking it, while keeping it safe. Keep a hamper where clothes come off.

Use open or visible storage if hidden objects disappear from your awareness. Use closed storage if visual clutter creates sensory pressure. The correct system is the one your brain can use, not the one that photographs well.

Housework can also have levels.

Minimum laundry may mean clean clothes remain in baskets.

Minimum dishes may mean washing only what is needed for the next meal or using disposable items temporarily where cost and waste considerations allow.

Minimum cleaning may mean rubbish, food safety, bathroom hygiene, and clear walking routes.

The home does not need to be finished. It needs to remain usable.

Money Problems Multiply Quietly

Burnout can increase spending and missed payments at the same time. Delivery food, taxis, duplicates, forgotten subscriptions, late fees, and urgent purchases may rise because the lower cost option requires more planning and effort.

Shame makes the problem harder to inspect.

Begin with protection.

1. Housing, utilities, food, medication, transport, and required insurance.
2. Automatic payments for stable essential bills where suitable.
3. Reminders several days before variable payments.
4. A short list of subscriptions and recurring charges.
5. One person or service to contact if paperwork becomes unmanageable.

Automation can help, but it can also create overdraft risk when income varies. Use it only where the timing and amount are predictable.

A "burnout budget" should include the cost of access. Ready meals may be more expensive than ingredients and still prevent food waste and missed meals. A taxi may preserve enough capacity for work. Paying for cleaning, if affordable, may remove a repeated crisis.

The cheapest option on paper can be the most expensive when it repeatedly fails.

Action Challenge: Protect One Financial Task

Choose the bill or process with the greatest consequence. Make one change. Use an automatic payment, calendar reminder, paper statement, password manager, trusted support, or benefits and debt advice.

Do not begin by cataloging every financial mistake. Protect the next consequence first.

Communication Can Use Shortcuts

Messages often fail because they require several decisions. You must decide what to say, how warm to sound, whether to explain, when to promise a reply, and how the other person might react.

Create three saved messages.

"I've seen this. I don't have capacity to reply properly today. I'll come back to it by Friday."

"I need to cancel. I'm dealing with a health and capacity problem and won't be able to attend."

"I can answer yes or no questions today, but I can't manage an open conversation."

Change the wording to sound like you. The shortcut should not create more explanation than you want to give.

A message can be brief without being cruel.

If you cannot promise a date, do not invent one. Say, "I will contact you when I can." For urgent practical matters, name another person or route if one exists.

Accept Support That Fits the Task

Support can come from partners, friends, relatives, colleagues, carers, community services, cleaners, delivery services, financial advisers, occupational therapists, support workers, or technology. Access depends on country, money, eligibility, and relationships.

The best support matches the barrier.

If initiation is missing, another person may begin beside you.

If sequence is missing, a written next step may help.

If decisions are missing, someone else can choose within agreed limits.

If sensory tolerance is the barrier, changing the environment matters more than encouragement.

If physical energy is severely reduced, the task may need to be done for you.

Support that asks you to perform the same inaccessible function is not well matched.

"Tell me every step" does not help when sequencing is the problem.

"Choose what I should cook" does not help when decisions are the problem.

"Call me if you need me" does not help when initiation and language are unavailable.

Specific support begins where access ends.

Create a Low Capacity Station

Choose one area from food, hygiene, medication, paperwork, or communication.

Place the necessary items together. Remove optional steps. Add a written instruction if useful. Include the minimum version first.

A hygiene station might contain wipes, deodorant, clean clothes, mouth care, and a bag for used items.

A paperwork station might contain unopened post, a bin for rubbish, a folder for action, stamps, passwords stored safely, and one note showing whom to contact.

A communication station might be a phone folder containing saved messages and emergency contacts.

Test the station on a low capacity day. If you do not use it, inspect the barrier. The system may be in the wrong place, contain too many choices, or still require an unavailable step.

The station should carry part of the task.

Body Care Without Moral Meaning

Daily care often carries moral language. Clean means good. Messy means careless. Cooking means responsible. Delivery means wasteful. Independence means adulthood. Needing help means failure.

These meanings make practical problems harder to solve.

A missed shower is information about access. A room full of packaging may show that food is arriving while cleanup has failed. Repeated clothes may reduce sensory decisions. None of these facts tells you what kind of person you are.

Address health, safety, comfort, cost, and consequence. Leave character out of the assessment.

Ask, “What is the smallest change that makes this safer or easier?” You may need a bin beside the bed, a chair in the bathroom, a laundry service, a friend to sit nearby, or professional support with daily living.

The correct level of help is the level that protects the outcome.

Create an Administration Window

Paperwork spreads because every envelope and message interrupts the day. An administration window contains the task.

Choose one short period each week. Gather post, bills, appointment messages, and forms in one place. Use three categories. Mark items urgent, waiting, or filed. Stop when the time ends unless a deadline requires action.

If paperwork is already severe, ask another person or advice service to help triage it. Do not begin by creating a perfect archive. Protect housing, income, healthcare, debt deadlines, and legal responsibilities first.

A 20 minute window can be more usable than carrying every unopened envelope mentally for seven days.

Plan for Supply Failure

Low capacity systems fail when the final item is used. The toothpaste, medication, safe food, clean underwear, or pet food runs out and creates an urgent multi step task.

Choose five essential supplies. Keep one backup where cost, storage, and safety allow. Add a reorder point before the backup is opened. If duplicates are not affordable, place the reminder earlier or ask someone else to monitor the item.

The purpose is not stockpiling. It is preventing an empty container from becoming a crisis.

Principles to Remember

A basic task can contain many sensory, decision, switching, and sequence demands.

Protect the outcome with minimum, supported, and standard versions.

Food needs to be accessible before hunger removes more capacity.

Medication systems should reduce forgetting and uncertainty without changing medical instructions.

The home can store the sequence through duplicates, visible placement, and fewer stages.

A burnout budget includes the cost of access, not only the cheapest theoretical option.

Support should match the missing access. Encouragement cannot replace a sequence, decision, sensory change, or transferred task.

Safe enough is a real standard.

Chapter 8: Work Without Pretending

The workday begins before the first task and ends after the body has recovered from it.

The cost of work includes everything required to reach, perform, display, switch, and recover from the role. A job can match your skills while the environment and working method remain unsustainable.

This chapter will help you separate the work from the job conditions, identify the real cost, request specific changes, and recognize when adjustment cannot repair a fundamental mismatch.

Audit the Whole Workday

Keira liked the work and dreaded the job.

She was a data analyst. Quiet concentration, complex patterns, and clear problems suited her. The work itself could hold her attention for hours.

The job included an open office, a commute, unexpected desk conversations, meetings with no agenda, changing priorities, and the expectation that cameras remained on during remote calls. Her manager praised her output and told her to "speak up more" in meetings. By the time Keira arrived home, she could not tolerate the sound of cutlery.

She assumed the career was wrong because she was exhausted by the workplace around it.

When she began separating the work from the job conditions, the problem became more precise. She did not need to abandon analysis. She needed fewer interruptions, clearer priorities, lower sensory input, and recovery between meetings.

Job descriptions list responsibilities. They rarely list the sensory and social method by which those responsibilities must be completed.

A work audit should include:

Travel and preparation

Lighting, sound, temperature, clothing, and physical space

Interruptions and switching

Meetings, small talk, phone calls, and video expectations

Clarity of instructions and priorities

Time pressure and unpredictable changes

Masking and emotional performance

Recovery required after the workday

Keira discovered that the commute and first hour in the office used more sensory capacity than three hours of analysis at home. She also found that two short meetings divided her best focus period into unusable fragments.

The task was not "work eight hours." It was "change environments, filter input, appear socially available, restart several times, complete technical work, then travel again."

As Chapter 2 showed, the calendar contained Visible Load while most of the work sat in Hidden Load.

Action Challenge: Complete the Work Cost Audit

For five workdays, record one sentence under each heading:

What gave me access?

What used the most capacity?

What cost arrived after work?

What condition could change without changing the actual job outcome?

Look for repeated conditions. A rare crisis may be less important than a daily meeting placed at the wrong time.

Adjustments Should Name Function

"Less stress" is understandable and difficult for a manager to implement.

Specific adjustments connect a barrier with a work outcome.

"I need written priorities after the meeting because verbal changes are difficult to retain accurately."

"I need two protected focus blocks without instant message interruptions so I can complete the report."

"I need access to a lower stimulus workspace because background speech prevents sustained concentration and causes headaches."

"I need meeting agendas in advance and permission to contribute in writing."

Research reviews and studies of autistic employment repeatedly identify clear communication, predictable duties, reduced distraction, lower noise, flexible schedules, and supportive attitudes as common forms of workplace accommodation (Khalifa et al., 2020; Petty et al., 2023).

Not every adjustment is possible in every role. The value of specificity remains. It allows a real decision instead of a general discussion about whether you are stressed enough.

Disclosure Is a Choice With Tradeoffs

You may disclose a diagnosis, describe a disability related need without naming every diagnosis, or request a working change through ordinary management channels. Laws and procedures differ by country. Seek local employment advice when rights or risk matter.

Disclosure can create access to formal adjustments and greater understanding. It can also expose a person to stigma, disbelief, reduced opportunities, or unwanted attention. Research on autistic workplace disclosure reports potential benefits and costs, with outcomes shaped heavily by organizational culture and manager response (Lindsay et al., 2021).

You do not owe every colleague your medical history.

Decide what the listener needs to know:

The barrier

The effect on work

The requested change

How the change supports the role

A diagnosis may be relevant to formal documentation. A team member may only need to know that written requests work better than verbal ones.

Tessa disclosed to her manager but not her wider team. Her manager arranged a quieter desk and allowed written follow-up after meetings. The team was told that Tessa's working arrangement had changed. She kept the private details private.

Disclosure should serve a purpose. It is not a test of honesty.

Remote Work Can Help and Harm

Remote work can reduce commuting, lighting, clothing, social monitoring, and background noise. It can also blur the workday, increase written messages, remove transition cues, and make it difficult to stop.

Keira initially worked longer at home because she used the absence of commuting as extra work time. She answered messages during meals and left her laptop open in the room where she recovered. The environment improved. The boundary disappeared.

She created an end sequence: write the next task, close every work application, put the laptop in a cupboard, change the light, and play the same song. The sequence replaced the commute as a transition.

Remote work is not automatically accommodating. It needs structure that protects stopping.

Meetings Are More Than Minutes

A 30 minute meeting may use several hours of capacity through preparation, anticipation, performance, switching, and recovery.

Reduce the extra cost where possible:

Ask for an agenda and desired decision.

Request optional camera use.

Contribute in writing.

Attend only the portion relevant to your role.

Place meetings together or protect space between them, depending on which creates less cost.

Use captions or written notes.

Clarify action owners before the meeting ends.

A meeting is useful when it changes a decision, coordinates work, or resolves uncertainty. A meeting that merely displays availability may be an expensive ritual.

You may not control whether it occurs. You can still ask what outcome requires your presence.

Protect the After Work Threshold

Many women use everything at work because work has immediate consequences. Home receives whatever remains.

The first period after work is therefore not empty. It is a threshold between roles. Filling it with questions, errands, childcare transfer, cooking decisions, or social contact can trigger a rapid collapse.

Protect 20 to 60 minutes where possible. The period may include transport in silence, changing clothes, food already chosen, darkness, movement, or no speech.

If you share a home, explain the function:

"When I arrive, I need 30 minutes without decisions or conversation. After that, I can tell you what is available."

This is not a demand that everyone disappear indefinitely. It is a planned transition that may return more access to the evening.

The most useful workplace adjustment may be one that protects life outside work.

Staged Return Needs Stages

Returning after leave can fail when the measure of success is simply presence.

A staged return may need changes in hours, task type, sensory environment, meeting load, decision complexity, and pace. Returning to four hours of the most demanding activity may cost more than six hours of quieter work.

Use a Return-to-Demand Ladder, developed fully in Chapter 12. For work, it might begin with familiar solo tasks, then limited meetings, then a longer day, then unpredictable or high social tasks.

Add one dimension at a time. Check the delayed cost before adding another.

A successful first week does not prove that all previous demands can return in week two.

When the Job Is the Mismatch

Some environments cannot or will not change enough.

A customer facing role may require continuous interaction. A shift job may remain unpredictable. A manager may reject workable requests or requests that may qualify for formal accommodation under local law. The organization may praise wellbeing while rewarding constant availability.

Do not call a structural mismatch a personal failure.

The decision to leave may still be complicated by money, healthcare, immigration status, identity, family, or the absence of another job. Recognizing the mismatch does not force an immediate exit. It allows a harm reduction plan while options are built.

Protect documents. Learn local rights. Record adjustment requests and responses. Seek union, disability, occupational health, legal, or employment support where available. Reduce nonessential load outside work while the fixed demand remains high.

A job can be unsustainable before you are ready to leave it.

Write the Adjustment Request

Use this structure:

"The current barrier is __________."

"It affects my work by __________."
"I am requesting __________."
"This would support the role by __________."
"For the next four weeks, we can assess it through __________."
Example:

"The current barrier is frequent unplanned interruption during technical work. It causes repeated restart time and errors. I am requesting two 90 minute focus blocks each day with messages paused except for urgent issues. This would support accurate completion of the monthly report. For four weeks, we can assess the change through completion times and error corrections."

Keep the request focused. A manager does not need the entire history of your burnout to understand the work condition.

Prepare the Manager Conversation

A manager may want to help and still respond poorly to a long, emotionally charged explanation delivered without a clear request. Prepare the conversation around work function.

Begin with the shared outcome. Name the barrier. Offer one or two changes. Suggest a review date.

"I want to keep producing accurate reports. Unplanned calls are breaking the focus time the report requires. I would like nonurgent questions collected in writing and a protected block from 10 to 12. Can we test that for four weeks?"

Bring notes. Send a written summary afterward. If the request involves formal disability rights, occupational health, or medical documentation, use the process required where you live.

You do not need to prove the full severity of your private collapse to justify a reasonable conversation about how work is completed.

Decide With More Than Exhaustion

Severe burnout can make every job look impossible. A brief improvement can make an unsuitable job look manageable again. Major career decisions deserve more than the highest or lowest day.

Separate the role into four questions:

Do I value or tolerate the actual work?

Can the environment change enough?

Can the schedule and recovery cost change enough?

What financial and practical runway exists for another option?

You may discover that the profession fits and the employer does not. The work fits and the hours do not. The role fits only with adjustments. Or the entire field now carries a cost you no longer want to pay.

Recognition does not require immediate resignation. Build information, support, savings where possible, references, and a transition plan.

Keep a Work Evidence Log

Record barriers, requested adjustments, agreed actions, and outcomes. Keep the tone factual. Dates, examples, and written follow-up protect memory and make later review easier.

The log can also reveal success. Fewer errors after written instructions, better output during focus blocks, or reduced sick days after sensory changes provide evidence that the adjustment supports the role.

The purpose is not to prepare for conflict in every workplace. It is to stop important agreements from depending on exhausted memory.

The Work-Cost Decision

The cost of work includes the environment, travel, masking, interruption, switching, and recovery.

A career can fit your skills while the job conditions remain harmful.

Specific adjustments name the barrier, work effect, requested change, and useful outcome.

Disclosure is a choice with benefits and risks. Share the information needed for the purpose.

Remote work needs an ending structure, not only a different location.

A staged return should add one type of demand at a time and measure delayed cost.

The value of work should not be measured only by whether you can survive the workday.

A job has taken too much when it consumes the life that pays for it.

Chapter 9: Capacity Across Hormonal Change

Tessa noticed the pattern only after her diagnosis.

For years, there were weeks when medication seemed less reliable, sleep became lighter, sounds felt sharper, and ordinary requests caused a physical sense of pressure. She often spent those days trying to repair her routines. New planner. Earlier bedtime. Stricter food rules. More exercise.

Then the pattern eased. Tessa concluded that the system had worked.

Several weeks later, the same collapse returned.

When she marked symptoms beside her menstrual cycle, she saw that some of the hardest periods clustered before menstruation. The pattern did not explain every crash. It did explain why a routine that worked for much of the month could suddenly require more effort.

Later, in her mid-forties, the timing became less predictable. Sleep changes, temperature shifts, and cognitive strain no longer followed the earlier rhythm. Tessa needed a new map.

Hormonal change may alter attention, mood, sleep, and perceived medication response for some women. Sensory tolerance may also shift for some individuals, but direct evidence is much thinner. Track patterns without assuming that hormones explain everything, and use the pattern to plan support and speak with an appropriate clinician.

The evidence in this area is developing.

The Research Has Gaps

Research on ADHD across menstrual cycles, pregnancy, postpartum periods, and menopause remains limited compared with the questions women bring to clinicians. A 2025 systematic review identified only 11 relevant studies and found evidence that was largely suggestive, with small samples and substantial variation in methods and participants (Osianlis et al., 2025). Narrative and theoretical reviews propose possible cycle-related changes in ADHD symptoms and treatment response, but they do not establish one universal pattern (Eng et al., 2024; Rapoport & Groenman, 2025; Wynchank et al., 2026).

Evidence specific to combined autism and ADHD is much thinner. Current research cannot provide a precise rule for AuDHD experiences at any hormonal life stage.

A careful chapter does not turn a plausible mechanism into a promise.

Use tracking to identify your own repeated pattern. Use clinical care to consider treatment, medication, and other medical causes.

Track Capacity, Not Only Symptoms

Symptom lists can become overwhelming. A capacity tracker asks what changed in daily access.

For eight weeks, record once per day or several times per week:

Menstrual cycle day or bleeding, if relevant

Sleep quality

Medication timing and perceived effect

Sensory tolerance

Starting and switching

Mood and emotional range

Appetite and food access

Speech and social tolerance

Pain, headaches, temperature symptoms, or other physical changes

Major demands

Use a simple scale such as higher, mixed, or lower. The tracker should take less than two minutes.

After two cycles, look for clusters. Do not force a pattern. Work deadlines, illness, sleep, conflict, and travel may explain more than cycle timing in a given month.

Action Challenge: Choose Three Variables

If a full tracker feels too large, choose three variables: cycle day, sleep, and one area of capacity that most affects life. Record them for eight weeks.

The smaller tracker you complete is more useful than the detailed tracker you abandon.

Plan for Predictable Narrowing

A repeated lower capacity window can be treated like a known environmental condition.

Reduce optional meetings.

Use more predictable food.

Protect sleep and transition time.

Avoid placing several high social events together.

Prepare medication questions for the prescriber.

Tell a partner which responsibilities may need transfer.

Keep the plan flexible. The aim is not to declare an entire week unusable. It is to stop planning the same load when the available number may be different.

Tessa moved her monthly reporting work earlier when possible. She also stopped scheduling family visits in the days when sensory tolerance was repeatedly lower. The change did not remove symptoms. It prevented the same symptom window from meeting the same peak workload.

Planning is easier when the pattern is treated as data rather than a character change.

Medication Questions Belong With the Prescriber

Some women report that stimulant effects feel different across the menstrual cycle. Reviews identify limited evidence of cycle-related changes in ADHD symptoms and perceived medication response, including reports of worsening during the luteal or premenstrual phase. The available studies are too small and heterogeneous to establish a standard dosing rule (Findeis & Strauß, 2025; Osianlis et al., 2025; Wynchank et al., 2026).

Do not increase, reduce, stop, or change prescribed medication because you notice a cycle pattern without speaking to the prescriber.

Bring the tracker. Ask:

"Could this pattern be related to hormonal change?"

"Are there other conditions or medication effects we should consider?"

"What options are evidence based for my situation?"

"What should I monitor if treatment changes?"

A good answer may include uncertainty. Uncertainty is not the same as dismissal.

If the clinician says there is no possible connection without reviewing the pattern, you may seek a second opinion where possible. If an online source promises an exact medication formula for every phase, be cautious.

Pregnancy Changes More Than Hormones

Pregnancy can alter sleep, appetite, nausea, pain, sensory experience, medication decisions, work, body awareness, and the number of medical appointments. The postpartum period can add sleep interruption, feeding demands, touch, noise, uncertainty, and near constant responsibility.

These changes may increase the Capacity Gap even when the pregnancy or new child is deeply wanted.

Medication decisions during pregnancy or breastfeeding require individualized advice from a prescriber, pharmacist, midwife, or other appropriately qualified professional. Do not start, stop, increase, or reduce prescribed medication from this book.

A pregnancy support plan can include:

Written questions for appointments

A person who attends and helps remember information

Reduced sensory exposure where possible

Practical food options

Clear ownership of night and household tasks

A postpartum plan that assumes lower capacity rather than waiting for collapse

The cultural story that a mother should instinctively cope can hide serious need. Ask for practical support before exhaustion becomes total.

If persistent low mood, severe anxiety, frightening thoughts, marked confusion, hallucinations, delusions, or inability to function appears during pregnancy or after birth, seek professional help promptly. Postnatal depression requires assessment, and postpartum psychosis is a medical emergency (National Health Service, 2023a; National Health Service, 2026a).

Perimenopause Can Change the Map

Perimenopause is the transition leading to menopause. It can involve changes in periods, sleep, hot flushes or temperature symptoms, mood, memory, concentration, and physical comfort (National Health Service, 2026b). These changes can interact with existing ADHD and autistic needs.

Qualitative research with neurodivergent women in the workplace has described menopause as intensifying difficulties and disrupting established ways of managing paid work for some participants (Gottardello & Steffan, 2024). The study does not prove that every change is caused by menopause. It does show why the intersection deserves attention.

A woman who built reliable systems around a predictable cycle may find that the pattern no longer holds. Sleep disruption may lower Available Capacity. Temperature sensitivity can make clothing and workplaces harder to tolerate. Memory complaints can increase anxiety about competence. Medication response may also feel different for some women, but direct evidence in perimenopause remains limited.

Do not assume that age makes every symptom normal. New cognitive, mood, sleep, bleeding, pain, or physical changes should be discussed with a clinician.

Yvonne had managed a senior role through years of ADHD difficulty by preparing early and working in long focused blocks. During perimenopause, sleep became unpredictable and the blocks failed. She initially responded by staying later. The extra hours worsened sleep and reduced sensory tolerance.

Her useful change was not a more forceful routine. She reduced morning meetings, worked from home after poor sleep when possible, and sought medical advice about the wider symptoms.

The old system was not proof of what she should still be able to do. It was a system built for different conditions.

Do Not Reduce Every Woman to Hormones

Hormonal explanations can be relieving. They can also be used to dismiss women.

A manager may hear "menopause" and ignore an unreasonable workload. A clinician may attribute every symptom to stress or hormones without assessment. A partner may treat predictable difficulty as irrationality.

The Capacity Gap Map keeps the picture wider.

Hormonal change may affect Available Capacity.

Work, masking, caregiving, sleep, pain, and sensory conditions still contribute Visible Load and Hidden Load.

Recovery Access still matters.

A cycle pattern does not make the environment irrelevant.

It also does not make your experience imaginary because the pattern changes.

Prepare the Clinical Conversation

Bring one page containing:

Your main symptoms

When they occur

Effect on daily life

Cycle or life stage pattern

Medication and supplements

Sleep changes

Relevant medical and family history

Questions you want answered

Use concrete examples. "I make more mistakes" becomes "I sent the wrong file twice in the week before menstruation for three cycles." "My medication stops working" becomes "I can begin tasks for most of the month, but initiation becomes much less reliable during these four days."

The examples do not prove a cause. They make the question assessable.

Treatment Decisions Need Individual Advice

General information about menstrual cycles, contraception, hormone therapy, pregnancy, and ADHD medication cannot tell you what is safe or appropriate for your body. Medical history, age, other medicines, pregnancy plans, cardiovascular risk, migraine, bleeding patterns, and many other factors can change the decision.

Bring observations rather than a proposed prescription.

"My sleep and initiation change during these days."

"These symptoms began after this treatment change."

"This pattern is affecting work and food access."

Ask what evidence supports the available options, what uncertainty remains, and what should be monitored. If hormone therapy, contraception, or medication is discussed, make sure the clinician knows the complete medication list and relevant medical history.

A treatment plan should be individualized. A social media schedule is not a substitute.

Adjust Work Before the Window

If a pattern is repeated, change the conditions before the lower capacity period begins.

Complete high uncertainty tasks earlier where possible. Ask for agendas. Prepare food. Reduce travel. Move difficult conversations. Protect the first evening after an office day. Tell the person who shares responsibility what may need transfer.

This is not surrender to a calendar. It is the same planning you would use around any predictable limit.

Some months will differ. Keep the plan light enough to adjust. The aim is a prepared option, not a rigid forecast.

When the Pattern Changes

A cycle that was predictable may change through stress, illness, contraception, pregnancy, postpartum recovery, perimenopause, medication, or age. Do not keep forcing the old explanation.

Return to the wider symptom timeline from Chapter 4. Note what changed, when, and what else was happening. Seek medical advice for unusual bleeding, severe pain, marked mood change, new physical symptoms, or another concern.

A tracker is most useful when it allows the model to change.

Principles to Remember

Hormonal change may affect attention, mood, sleep, and perceived medication response for some women. Sensory changes may occur, but direct AuDHD evidence is limited.

Research is developing and does not support one universal cycle rule.

Track capacity and context, not only symptoms.

Use repeated lower capacity windows to adjust load before the crash.

Medication changes belong with the prescriber.

Pregnancy and postpartum periods change sleep, sensory input, appointments, responsibility, and medication decisions as well as hormones.

Perimenopause may require a new operating plan when older systems stop fitting.

Hormones can affect the Capacity Gap. They do not explain the whole map.

Chapter 10: Share the Weight

Hannah's partner said he was willing to help.

He meant it. If she asked him to collect a prescription, he did. If she sent a shopping list, he bought the items. If she told him which school message needed an answer, he replied.

Hannah still held the household in her head.

She noticed when the food was running out, remembered the medical forms, checked the school calendar, chose the birthday gifts, knew which clothes no longer fitted, and decided what needed to happen next. Her partner performed tasks. Hannah remained the person responsible for seeing them.

During burnout, the difference became impossible to ignore. She could not keep producing instructions. Her partner felt rejected because she stopped speaking. Hannah felt abandoned because nobody acted until she spoke.

They were both waiting for the wrong kind of communication.

Relationships reduce burnout only when responsibility, communication, and expectations change in practical ways. Support is not agreement that you are struggling. It is effort that no longer has to pass through you.

This chapter is about partners, relatives, friends, adult children, and other close relationships. It cannot make an unwilling person fair. It can help you make the needed change specific enough to test.

Help and Ownership Differ

Help begins after you identify and assign the task. Ownership begins before that point.

Ownership includes noticing, planning, remembering, doing, checking, and repairing. If the laundry turns pink, the owner solves it. If the food is unavailable, the owner changes the plan. If an appointment moves, the owner updates the calendar.

Hannah and her partner listed the repeated household areas rather than individual chores. Food. School. Laundry. Bills. Cleaning. Health appointments. Family communication.

Her partner took full ownership of food for four weeks. That meant checking supplies, planning within agreed preferences and budget, shopping, deciding dinner, and handling cleanup. Hannah could still express a need. She no longer had to operate the system.

The first week felt uncomfortable. Her partner bought different yogurt and served dinner later than Hannah preferred. She had to decide whether difference was a genuine access problem or the discomfort of no longer controlling the method.

Ownership requires room for another competent adult to do the task differently.

It does not require tolerating unsafe, careless, or deliberately poor work. The standard is agreed outcome, not identical process.

Action Challenge: Transfer a Domain

Choose one repeated domain. Write the outcome, important limits, and duration of the transfer.

Example:

"For the next two weeks, you own weekday dinner. The limits are our budget, the allergy list, and food being available by seven. You choose the meals, shop, cook or order, and clean up. I will tell you if a sensory need changes, but I won't direct each step."

A trial period makes the change easier to assess.

Reduced Speech Needs a Plan

When language access drops, relationships can become more demanding at the exact moment you have less capacity.

The other person may ask more questions because they are worried. You may answer less because each question requires interpretation and reassurance. They may read silence as anger. You may experience their need for clarity as pressure.

Prepare a low language plan when both people are calm.

Choose one signal for overload.

Agree what it means.

Agree what the other person should do.

Agree when contact will resume.

Hannah used a message saved on her phone:

"I'm overloaded and speech is limited. I'm not ending the relationship or refusing the issue. Please give me 45 minutes without questions. If something is urgent, send one yes or no question."

The message did not solve every disagreement. It prevented overload from becoming a debate about whether Hannah cared.

A person can need information without being entitled to receive it at the moment your language disappears.

Ask for Actions, Not Atmosphere

"I need more support" describes a real need but does not tell another person what changes.

Try asking for observable actions:

"Please make the appointment and tell me the time."

"When I come home, please wait 30 minutes before asking about dinner."

"If plans change, text me the new time rather than telling me while I'm doing something else."

"Please take over the conversation with the school for this month."

"I need you to believe me without asking for a full explanation each time."

The last request is also observable. The other person can respond, "Okay. What is the next practical step?" instead of requiring proof.

Specificity does not guarantee cooperation. It reveals whether cooperation exists.

Social Contact Can Change Shape

Burnout may reduce the frequency, length, and type of contact you can manage. Friends may assume reduced contact means reduced affection. You may disappear because explaining the change feels too difficult.

A short message can protect the relationship:

"I'm in a low capacity period. I care about you, but conversation and plans are difficult. Please keep sending ordinary things without expecting quick replies."

Some friendships can shift to quieter forms: voice notes without deadlines, parallel activities, shorter visits, walks without intense conversation, or contact based on a shared interest.

Other friendships depend on immediate response, long events, or emotional availability you cannot currently provide. Burnout can reveal that the relationship worked partly because you carried the adaptation.

That realization may hurt. It does not require an immediate verdict. Test a smaller form of contact and see whether the relationship can adjust.

A friend who values you may still need time to understand. A friend who repeatedly punishes reduced capacity is giving you different information.

Touch and Intimacy Need Current Consent

During periods of severe overload, some people report that touch which is usually comforting becomes painful, startling, or overwhelming. Reduced speech, exhaustion, and lower tolerance for interaction may also change what intimacy is available.

Do not promise the future version of your capacity to reduce discomfort in the present conversation.

Say what is available now:

"I want closeness, but I can't tolerate light touch tonight. Firm pressure may be okay."

"I don't want sexual contact. I can sit beside you for 20 minutes."

"I need to sleep alone tonight because movement and sound are keeping me alert."

A partner is allowed to have feelings about change. They are not allowed to treat consent as a debt created by the relationship.

Intimacy can include practical care, shared humor, quiet company, planned touch, affection without escalation, and honest limits.

Repair After Overload

Burnout can make you more abrupt. You may leave a room, miss a promise, speak sharply, or shut down during a difficult conversation. Neurodivergence explains context. It does not erase impact.

Repair works best when it is specific and does not require self-destruction.

"I spoke harshly when you asked about the bill. That hurt you. I was overloaded, but the tone was still mine. Next time I will use the saved message and return to the conversation after dinner."

Avoid an apology that becomes a demand for the other person to reassure you.

"I am the worst person, you should leave me" turns their hurt into another situation they must manage.

Also avoid accepting blame for having a limit.

"I am sorry I needed quiet" is different from "I am sorry I shouted."

You can repair behavior without apologizing for capacity.

Misunderstanding and Refusal Differ

A person may not understand AuDHD burnout at first. They may need concrete examples, written information, or time to adjust habits.

Refusal looks different.

They agree in calm conversations and repeatedly ignore the plan.

They call accommodations selfish.

They deliberately increase sensory or social pressure to prove a point.

They use your diagnosis to dismiss every disagreement.

They punish you for reduced speech, boundaries, or medical needs.

They make help dependent on gratitude, obedience, or access to your body.

If a relationship is controlling, frightening, or abusive, a communication script is not the main intervention. Seek confidential local support and consider safety before confrontation. Do not announce plans that could increase danger.

The fact that burnout makes conflict harder does not mean you caused the conditions around you.

Family Roles May Need Grief

Some relationships were built around you as the reliable daughter, social organizer, calm partner, available friend, or endlessly capable mother. Reducing the role can feel like losing part of your place in the family.

Other people may grieve too. They may miss traditions, availability, or the version of the relationship that depended on your overfunctioning.

Grief does not automatically mean the change is wrong.

You can keep the value while changing the method. A family celebration becomes lunch rather than an evening event. You remember birthdays but no longer organize every gift. You stay connected with a parent without answering daily calls. You remain loving while refusing to be the only person who notices.

A relationship can survive disappointment. It cannot remain sustainable if one person must repeatedly collapse to maintain it.

Write the Support Agreement

Create a one page agreement with a partner, relative, or close friend. Include:

Early signs you are losing capacity
The signal you will use
What support helps
What makes overload worse
Which responsibilities transfer
When you will review the plan

Keep it practical. "Be patient" becomes "ask one question at a time." "Give space" becomes "no conversation for 30 minutes unless there is immediate danger."

An agreement does not remove the need for flexibility. It removes some decisions from the hardest moment.

Caregiving Needs Backup Ownership

Parents and carers may not be able to withdraw when capacity falls. Children, disabled relatives, older family members, and animals still need care.

A backup plan should name people and tasks before a crisis. Who can collect? Who can prepare food? Who knows medication, school, or care routines? Which standards can temporarily fall? Which responsibilities require professional or emergency support if no informal help exists?

Do not describe a backup person as "helping with the children." Name the period and ownership.

"From five to bedtime, you own food, homework messages, and the bedtime sequence. Contact me only for immediate safety or health decisions."

If you are the only available carer and your functioning is no longer sufficient for safety, seek urgent practical support through family, health, social care, school, community, or emergency routes available where you live.

Needing backup does not cancel love. It recognizes that dependents need a system larger than one exhausted person.

Let Friends Know the New Shape

A friendship update can be brief and specific:

"I have less capacity for spontaneous calls. Text first."

"I can meet for one hour in a quiet place, but evenings are not working."

"I may read messages without replying. Please do not treat that as a hidden conflict."

"I want invitations even when I often decline."

The other person is allowed preferences too. Some forms of friendship may not fit both people. Honest limits give the relationship a chance to find out.

Stop Making Every Conversation Immediate

Important issues do not always need immediate processing. During overload, urgency can make both people less accurate.

Agree on a return time:

"We will discuss the bill tomorrow at 11."

"We will write our main points before the conversation."

"We will stop after 30 minutes and decide whether another conversation is needed."

A delayed conversation should not become indefinite avoidance. A scheduled return lowers immediate pressure while preserving trust.

Principles to Remember

Support is effort that no longer has to pass through you.

Help completes a task you identified. Ownership includes noticing, planning, remembering, doing, and repairing.

Prepare low language communication before speech disappears.

Ask for actions rather than a general atmosphere of support.

Friendship can change form without ending.

Repair harmful behavior without apologizing for having a limit.

Misunderstanding may improve with information and practice. Repeated refusal gives you different information.

A relationship is not sustainable when your collapse is part of its operating system.

Chapter 11: Unmask With Care

Unmasking is not the same as disclosure, and neither requires removing every protective strategy at once.

Selective Unmasking means reducing specific masking behaviors where doing so is safe, useful, and proportionate. It is not a duty to reveal every trait, disclose every diagnosis, or remove every protection at once.

Masking can be costly. It can also serve real functions. A careful approach respects both facts.

Masking Is More Than Pretending

Imani stopped making eye contact at work on Monday.

She had read that masking contributed to burnout and decided she was finished. She wore headphones at her desk, moved when she needed to move, answered questions directly, and declined lunch in the shared kitchen.

By Wednesday, a colleague asked whether she was angry. Her manager said her communication felt abrupt. Imani went home furious that people preferred the performance. She also felt exposed. She had removed several strategies at once without deciding which changes were safe, useful, or likely to be understood.

The lesson was not that unmasking had failed. The experiment had no ladder.

Masking may include suppression, compensation, imitation, rehearsal, and concealment. It can affect movement, facial expression, speech, interests, sensory responses, communication style, clothing, and requests for support.

Some actions are conscious. Others have become automatic through years of correction and observation.

Research describes camouflaging as motivated by connection, safety, employment, and the wish to avoid stigma. Higher camouflaging is associated with anxiety, depression, lower self-esteem, reduced authenticity, exhaustion, and other negative consequences, although much of the evidence is cross-sectional and cannot establish a simple causal pathway (Cage & Troxell-Whitman, 2019; Evans et al., 2024; Klein et al., 2025).

This creates a real tension. “Stop masking” can sound freeing while ignoring employment, culture, race, gender, family, and safety. “Keep doing what works” can sound practical while ignoring the accumulated cost.

Selective Unmasking asks three questions:

What is this behavior protecting?

What is it costing?

What smaller change could preserve safety while reducing cost?

Start With the Masking Tax

Return to the Masking Tax Audit from Chapter 3. Choose one behavior with a high repeated cost.

Imani noticed that eye contact was not the largest cost. The largest cost was pretending to understand vague verbal instructions, then spending hours reconstructing the task alone. Reducing eye contact created attention without solving the main problem.

Her first useful change was to say, “I understand the goal, but I need the priorities in writing before I begin.”

That sentence reduced uncertainty, memory effort, and the risk of mistakes. It did not require disclosing her diagnosis.

The most visible mask is not always the most expensive one.

Action Challenge: Choose One Behavior

Write one masking behavior under each heading:

Protection it provides

Cost it creates

People and places where it feels necessary

People and places where it may be reduced

One small experiment

Test one behavior for one week. Do not change several high risk behaviors at once.

Use the Selective Unmasking Ladder

The **Selective Unmasking Ladder** has five levels.

Private recognition: Notice the behavior and its cost without changing it yet.

Private accommodation: Change your home, clothing, sensory environment, or routine where nobody else needs an explanation.

Trusted experiment: Reduce the behavior with one safe person or in one low risk setting.

Functional request: Ask for a change that reduces masking without sharing more personal information than necessary.

Open disclosure: Share diagnosis or identity where the purpose, risks, and likely support have been considered.

You may remain at one level for a long time. You may use different levels in different settings. The ladder is not a measure of courage.

Farah used private accommodation at home by changing clothes immediately and allowing movement while talking. With a close friend, she asked for direct questions rather than hints. At work, she made functional requests for written agendas. She chose not to disclose her diagnosis to the wider team.

Her life became less performative without becoming fully public.

Reduce Automatic Performance Gently

Automatic masking may become visible through body signals. Your shoulders rise. Your hands stop moving. Your voice becomes brighter. You smile while confused. You agree before you have processed the request.

Choose a physical cue that reminds you to pause.

Feet on the floor.

One slower breath.

Hands allowed to move under the table.

A note saying, "You can ask for time."

Then use a prepared sentence:

"I need a moment to process that."

"Please send the details."

"I don't know yet."

"I can answer tomorrow."

These sentences create a small gap between automatic performance and actual consent.

The goal is not perfect awareness. It is one more chance to notice what you are agreeing to.

Disclosure Is Not Unmasking's Final Stage

A person can disclose a diagnosis and continue masking heavily. Another person can reduce masking without naming autism or ADHD.

Disclosure is an information decision. Unmasking is a change in behavior, environment, and self-monitoring. They overlap but are not the same.

Before disclosing, ask:

What outcome do I want?

Who will receive the information?

What can they do with it?

Is there a record?

What support exists if the response is poor?

Can I request the change without full disclosure?

Disclosure may bring relief or clearer communication for some people, but it can also bring stigma or loss of privacy. Camouflaging research shows that people often mask in response to social pressure, stigma, and perceived risk, rather than because they have failed to accept themselves (Bradley et al., 2021; Tamura et al., 2025).

The environment has responsibilities too.

Expect Mixed Feelings

Reducing masking can produce relief and grief.

You may notice preferences you ignored. You may feel angry about years spent performing. You may become less tolerant of situations that once seemed manageable because you are no longer numbing the cost.

People around you may say you have become "more autistic" or "more difficult" after diagnosis. Sometimes the traits are more visible because you recognize them, stop suppressing them, or reach a period when suppression is no longer sustainable. During severe exhaustion, some people also report having less capacity to maintain familiar masking strategies.

Craddock's qualitative work with women diagnosed with autism and ADHD in adulthood describes the complexity of reinterpreting identity and occupying a combined diagnostic space not formally represented as one category (Craddock, 2026).

You do not have to turn the diagnosis into a complete explanation of who you are.

Identity can remain unfinished.

Watch for Unmasking as Another Standard

A new community can create new performance rules.

You may start monitoring whether you are stimming enough, resting correctly, disclosing bravely, using the right language, rejecting productivity, or appearing visibly neurodivergent. The old mask changes costume.

Ask whether a choice reduces monitoring or adds it.

You are allowed to enjoy conventional clothes, eye contact, schedules, social events, ambition, or polished communication. The question is not whether a behavior looks neurotypical. The question is whether it is chosen, accessible, and worth its cost.

A behavior does not become false because other people also do it.

When Unmasking Reveals a Bad Fit

A small change may reveal that the setting cannot tolerate difference.

You ask for written instructions and are mocked.

You wear ear protection and are treated as unprofessional.

You stop attending every family event and are accused of disloyalty.

You communicate directly and the relationship depends on guessing.

The experiment has produced information.

Do not immediately conclude that you must leave. Consider safety, rights, money, support, and whether the response can change. The information still matters. You now know that part of the previous fit depended on Hidden Load you supplied.

An environment that works only when you hide every cost is not a neutral environment.

Build the Ladder

Choose one repeated masking behavior. Write a five step ladder from private recognition to the highest level you may want. The final step does not have to be disclosure.

Example:

Notice that I agree before processing.

Use a private note that says "pause."

Practice "I'll answer tomorrow" with a friend.

Use the sentence in low risk work requests.

Ask my manager to make nonurgent decisions in writing.

Test one step. Record the result in terms of cost, safety, and access.

Did you have more energy afterward?

Did the change create conflict?

Did the conflict come from unclear communication, habit, or refusal?

What support would make the next step safer?

Unmasking is not a dramatic reveal. It is a series of informed choices.

Safety Is Shaped by Context

The risk of being read as rude, unstable, difficult, or unprofessional is not distributed evenly. Race, culture, class, gender expression, immigration status, age, visible disability, and workplace power can affect what happens when a person changes her communication or presentation.

Advice to "be yourself" can ignore those consequences.

Use the Selective Unmasking Ladder with the actual setting in mind. A behavior that is safe with a close friend may carry a different risk with a police officer, clinician, employer, landlord, or unfamiliar group. You are not less genuine because you make a safety calculation.

Where possible, reduce cost through changes that do not rely on other people interpreting you generously. Comfortable clothing under formal clothes, written instructions, planned breaks, private movement, quieter routes, and prepared language may protect capacity without making you more exposed.

Open expression is valuable. Safety remains valuable too.

Unmask at Home Without Transferring Harm

Home may be the first place you stop controlling movement, speech, facial expression, or sensory responses. Relief can be substantial. The people around you may also need information about what changes mean.

Reduced performance does not permit shouting, intimidation, insults, or controlling other people. It can include less eye contact, less small talk, direct language, movement, ear protection, separate sleep, repeated food, and leaving a room before overload becomes harmful.

Explain the behavior while capacity is available:

"When I leave without speaking, I am reducing overload. I will send a message when I can discuss the issue."

"When my face looks flat, please use my words rather than assuming anger."

"When I move during conversation, I am still listening."

Unmasking at home works best when it reduces performance without making everyone else responsible for guessing.

Keep a Choice Log

For one week, record one moment when you noticed a choice between performance and access. Write what you chose and what followed.

You may discover that some masking feels neutral, some protects something important, and some creates a large delayed cost. The log keeps the process specific.

The goal is not zero masking. It is fewer automatic payments you never agreed to make.

Your Selective Unmasking Rules

Selective Unmasking reduces specific masking behaviors where the change is safe, useful, and proportionate.

Masking may purchase safety, employment, privacy, and connection. Its function and cost both matter.

The most visible mask is not always the most expensive one.

Use a ladder: private recognition, private accommodation, trusted experiment, functional request, and open disclosure.

Disclosure and unmasking are related but different.

Relief can arrive beside grief, anger, and greater awareness of cost.

Do not turn unmasking into a new performance standard.

The safest change is not always the smallest. It is the change whose purpose and risk you understand.

Chapter 12: Rebuild Without Repeating

Zoe felt better on a Tuesday and spent the improvement by Wednesday.

She answered every delayed message, cleaned the kitchen, booked two appointments, accepted weekend plans, and told her manager she could return to normal hours. The activity felt wonderful. Her thoughts were clearer. Music sounded good again. She wanted her life back.

On Thursday, she woke with the old heaviness. By Friday, speech was difficult and she cancelled the weekend plans she had made during the burst.

Zoe concluded that recovery had been imaginary.

It was not imaginary. It was unprotected.

Rebuilding begins when a small amount of capacity can remain stable before more demand is added. Improvement is information, not an instruction to restore every postponed responsibility.

The task now is to build a **Capacity Floor**, the stable level of daily functioning protected before optional load returns.

Energy and Durable Capacity Differ

A burst of energy may come from interest, relief, urgency, medication timing, improved sleep, or the excitement of feeling more like yourself. Durable capacity shows itself through repetition and recovery.

Ask three questions before adding a demand:

Can I do it?

Can I recover from doing it?

Can I repeat it without losing basic care?

The first question is the one most people ask. The other two determine whether rebuilding lasts.

A social evening may be possible. If it removes food and speech access for two days, it may not yet be repeatable at the desired frequency. A four hour work block may be successful. If it makes sleep and hygiene unreliable, the return stage may be too high.

Possibility is not the same as readiness.

Establish the Capacity Floor

The **Capacity Floor** is this book's planning term for the smallest stable set of daily functions you protect before adding demand. It is not a clinical measure.

It may include:

Regular access to enough food and drink

Essential medication taken reliably

A workable sleep pattern

Basic hygiene in minimum or supported form

One period of Recovery Access each day

Ability to meet fixed responsibilities without repeated crisis

Some access to interest, connection, or pleasure

The floor is not an ideal life. It is the base that should remain when a new demand is tested.

If adding the gym removes food preparation, the floor has been breached. If returning to five workdays removes sleep and all weekend function, the floor has been breached. If a family visit makes medication unreliable, the floor has been breached.

The new activity may be valuable. The timing or dose may be wrong.

Action Challenge: Define Five Floor Signs

Write five signs that tell you your base remains stable. Make them observable.

"Coping well" is vague.

"Eating at least two adequate meals most days" is observable.

"Not too tired" is vague.

"Can answer one necessary message and prepare for sleep" is observable.

Review the signs after each new demand.

Add One Dimension at a Time

A demand has several dimensions: duration, frequency, sensory intensity, social complexity, uncertainty, travel, and recovery time.

Do not increase all of them together.

If you return to work, increase hours before adding several meetings. If you resume exercise, keep the location and routine familiar. If you return to social contact, choose a trusted person and a shorter event before a crowded celebration.

This approach may feel slower than your motivation. It gives the Capacity Gap Map enough time to show the delayed cost.

Dalia returned to a weekly art group. She first attended for 45 minutes, used her own materials, and left before the busy cleanup. After three weeks without losing her Capacity Floor, she stayed longer. She did not also add a second group, volunteer role, and evening class.

The activity became part of life instead of a test she had to pass.

Track Delayed Cost

Use a simple 48-hour observation window after adding something. This is a practical check, not a medical test or validated pacing rule:

Speech
Food
Sleep
Sensory tolerance
Starting and switching
Mood and interest
Body symptoms
Fixed responsibilities

Mark each as stable, strained, or lost.

A strained area is not automatic failure. It may mean the dose needs adjustment. Lost access to several floor functions means the stage is too high or recovery support is too low.

This check builds on the aftermath tracking from Chapter 1. You are no longer asking whether the activity was good or bad. You are asking what form and frequency your current capacity can support.

Build the Return-to-Demand Ladder

The **Return-to-Demand Ladder** is a staged process for adding responsibilities after stabilization.

Create four stages.

Stage one: familiar, low uncertainty, low social demand, easy to stop.

Stage two: longer duration or moderate complexity, with protected recovery.

Stage three: increased frequency, social demand, travel, or unpredictability.

Stage four: high consequence or high complexity demands, added only after lower stages remain stable.

For work, stage one may be familiar solo tasks at home. Stage two may add one meeting. Stage three may add office attendance. Stage four may restore crisis work or full responsibility.

For social life, stage one may be text contact. Stage two may be a short visit. Stage three may be a group. Stage four may be travel or hosting.

For household tasks, stage one may be one load of laundry with support. Stage two may add sorting. Stage three may add a second routine. Stage four may include a larger project.

The ladder should fit the domain. It should also contain a way back down.

Stepping down is not starting again. It is using the system.

Flexible Structure Serves Both Needs

Rigid routines can reduce decisions and uncertainty. They can also create pressure and boredom. Complete freedom can provide novelty while increasing choices, transitions, and unfinished tasks.

AuDHD often needs flexible structure.

Use fixed anchors with variable content.

The anchor may be eating within a time window. The content can come from three options.

The anchor may be a work start ritual. The first task can vary according to priority and interest.

The anchor may be Sunday planning. The plan includes protected open space.

Use predictable choice rather than a single rule or unlimited options.

Zoe created two morning versions. On higher capacity days, she showered, ate breakfast, and walked to a café before work. On lower capacity days, she used minimum hygiene, ate a prepared food, and worked from a quiet room. Both versions led to the same first work block.

Flexibility was built into the structure before the difficult morning arrived.

Pleasure Belongs in the Base

Recovery plans can become entirely defensive. Reduce noise. Cancel plans. Avoid overload. Protect sleep. Complete essentials.

Those actions may be necessary. A life made entirely of prevention is not the final aim.

Interest, pleasure, connection, movement, creativity, humor, and competence can be part of a usable life. Research with autistic adults suggests that special interests can support subjective wellbeing, although extremely intense engagement may also carry costs (Grove et al., 2018). These parts of life do not all need to be delayed until you are "fully recovered."

Include one low cost source of pleasure in the Capacity Floor. It may be a familiar book, music, a collection, time outside, contact with one person, a game, a pet, or an interest.

Pleasure is not proof that you are no longer burnt out. It is part of the life recovery is meant to protect.

Grieve the Old Operating Model

You may recover and still decide not to return to the old pace.

That decision can feel like loss. The old model may have produced achievement, income, praise, identity, and belonging. It may also have relied on emergency activation, masking, skipped meals, weekend collapse, and the belief that future you would pay the bill.

You do not have to call the old model entirely bad. It may have helped you survive or succeed. It may no longer be affordable.

The new model can include ambition. It requires a different funding source: clearer priorities, support, environmental fit, rest, and honest limits.

A sustainable life is not one in which nothing difficult happens. It is one in which difficulty does not repeatedly erase your access to the rest of life.

Review Before You Add

Before adding a demand, complete this sentence:

"I am adding __________ because __________."

"The floor I will protect is __________."

"The recovery condition is __________."

"I will review the delayed cost after __________."

"If the floor is breached, I will __________."

This short plan interrupts the rush created by improvement.

It does not remove spontaneity. It protects you from turning relief into a backlog emergency.

Expect Plateaus

Recovery may stop improving for a period. The plateau can mean the current conditions are supporting stability but not expansion. It can also mean illness, depression, sleep, pain, medication, hormones, or another factor needs review.

Do not respond automatically by pushing harder.

Check the Capacity Gap Map. Has Visible Load increased? Is Hidden Load still uncounted? Has Recovery Access remained protected? Are the minimum systems working? Has a new physical or mental health concern appeared?

A plateau is a point for assessment, not proof that you are lazy or permanently stuck.

Sometimes the next improvement comes from more time at the current stage. Sometimes it comes from a medical review, a workplace change, a transferred responsibility, or accepting that the target itself needs to change.

Respond to a Breached Floor

If a new demand breaches the Capacity Floor, act quickly.

Pause the added demand where possible. Return to the previous ladder stage. Restore food, medication, sleep, communication, and Recovery Access. Record which dimension created the cost: duration, frequency, sensory input, social complexity, uncertainty, travel, or inadequate recovery.

Do not punish yourself by removing every valued activity. Adjust the dose or conditions first.

Dalia's art group became too expensive when the room moved to a brighter, noisier venue. The activity had not suddenly become wrong for her. The sensory dimension changed. She tried ear protection, a seat near the door, and a shorter visit before deciding whether the group still fitted.

A breached floor gives information about the stage and setting.

Build Slack Into the Week

A plan filled to the exact edge of capacity fails when anything changes. Slack is unassigned room for delays, illness, transitions, and ordinary life.

Leave one evening without fixed plans. Avoid placing every important task on the same day. Keep simple food for the week when shopping fails. Finish a high consequence task before the final possible hour where your circumstances allow.

Slack can feel inefficient because it is visible as unused time. Its purpose becomes clear when the unexpected arrives and does not immediately become a crisis.

Capacity spent before the interruption cannot be spent twice.

Keep a Recovery Reserve

A rebuilding plan needs capacity that is not already promised. Call this your Recovery Reserve: time and access kept available after an activity so the cost can arrive without immediately damaging food, sleep, work, or communication.

The reserve does not have to be a whole empty day. It may be a quiet hour after an appointment, a simpler dinner after travel, no social plan on the evening after an office day, or someone else owning the morning routine after a late event. The useful amount depends on the demand and on your current Capacity Floor.

Before adding something, ask what will absorb the delayed cost. If the honest answer is skipped meals, lost sleep, cancelled essentials, or another person quietly covering the damage, the activity is not yet funded. You can change the timing, reduce the dose, add support, or wait.

Keira could attend a two hour training session, but the training became repeatable only when she stopped placing errands afterward and arranged a ready meal. The new activity did not require more determination. It required somewhere for the cost to go.

A Recovery Reserve makes rebuilding slower on paper and more durable in real life.

Principles to Remember

Improvement is information, not an instruction to restore every demand.

Ask whether an activity is possible, recoverable, and repeatable.

Protect a Capacity Floor before adding optional load.

Increase one dimension at a time: duration, frequency, sensory intensity, social complexity, uncertainty, or travel.

Use a 48-hour observation window to notice delayed cost, while remembering that the timing is a practical prompt rather than a medical rule.

Use a Return-to-Demand Ladder with a planned way to step down.

Flexible structure combines fixed anchors with limited choice.

The life you rebuild should contain something worth protecting, not only fewer ways to collapse.

Chapter 13: Catch the Crash Earlier

Early warning signs are useful only when they appear before your worst symptoms.

Look for small, observable changes across five areas. Track body, thinking, sensory tolerance, communication, and daily living. Shorter messages, narrower food choices, slower preparation, rigid routines, or reduced tolerance for ordinary input can matter before exhaustion becomes obvious.

The Early Warning Window is the period when your personal signs of rising load and narrowing access are present but severe collapse may still be prevented or reduced. A prevention system decides in advance what changes when those signs appear.

Autistic burnout research describes cumulative demands, masking, inadequate support, and limited recovery as recurring contributors, and reports that burnout may be prolonged or recurrent (Ali et al., 2025; Mantzalas et al., 2022; Raymaker et al., 2020). The prevention system in this chapter translates those broad findings into an author-created planning tool.

You will not prevent every crash. Health, grief, work, discrimination, caregiving, and sudden events can overwhelm even a careful system. The plan reduces delay and confusion. It does not promise control over everything.

Choose Early Signs, Not Worst Signs

Aisha's first sign was not tiredness.

It was punctuation.

Her messages became shorter. She stopped using greetings. She reread other people's replies and heard criticism that might not be there. At work, she began answering quickly because holding a request in mind felt unbearable. At home, she became rigid about meal times and felt panicked when plans shifted.

By the time exhaustion became obvious, the pattern had been active for weeks.

Aisha used to wait for certainty. She would not reduce work or cancel a plan until she could prove that burnout had arrived. Certainty came only after basic functions were lost.

Prevention began when she treated the earlier changes as enough information to act.

"Unable to work" is important and late.

"Using twice as long to prepare for meetings" is earlier.

"Stopped cooking" is important and late.

"Food choices narrowed and shopping became harder" is earlier.

"Cannot speak" is important and late.

"Messages became unusually brief and calls felt impossible" is earlier.

Return to the burnout sign list from Chapter 1. Choose signs that appear before major loss of function.

Use five areas.

Body

Thinking

Sensory tolerance

Communication

Daily living

Aisha's early signs included jaw pain, increased mistakes, clothing irritation, abrupt messages, and buying food without preparing it. No single sign proved burnout. Three signs appearing together triggered the plan.

The threshold should be clear enough to use when judgment is strained.

Build a Three Level System

Create three levels.

Green means stable enough. The Capacity Floor is mostly intact. Normal supports continue.

Amber means the Early Warning Window is open. Several early signs are present. Optional demand reduces and Recovery Access increases.

Red means severe loss of access or safety concern. The Minimum Viable Day begins, support is contacted, and medical or urgent help is used where needed.

This is a personal planning tool, not a diagnostic scale or emergency triage system. When safety or urgent medical concerns arise, use appropriate professional or emergency help rather than waiting for a color threshold.

Avoid using green to mean limitless. Stable capacity still has limits.

For each level, define actions.

At amber, Aisha cancelled one optional event, used prepared food, moved one meeting, stopped volunteering for new tasks, and protected an hour after work.

At red, she used a saved work message, contacted her sister, reduced the day to essentials, and arranged professional assessment if physical or mood symptoms were new or worsening.

The plan acted before she had to invent it.

Action Challenge: Write the Amber Rule

Complete this sentence.

"When I notice __________, __________, and __________ within one week, I will reduce __________ and protect __________ for seven days."

Make the response automatic enough that you do not have to argue with yourself.

Use the Capacity Gap Map Weekly

The Capacity Gap Map becomes most useful when it is brief.

Once a week, write the following.

Largest Visible Load

Largest Hidden Load

Area of lowest Available Capacity

Missing Recovery Access

One lever to use

This should take five minutes. A beautiful tracker is not required.

Look ahead for pressure clusters, including travel, school holidays, deadlines, family events, medical appointments, hormonal windows, financial dates, or several social obligations.

The aim is not to make life perfectly even. It is to stop surprise at a week that was visibly crowded before it began.

A predictable hard week can include prearranged food, fewer optional meetings, transferred household tasks, and protected recovery. Preparation does not remove the demand. It prevents every support decision from arriving after capacity is gone.

Plant Agreements Before Crisis

Other people need to know what changes when you enter amber or red.

A partner can own dinner and childcare transitions.

A manager can receive a short message requesting temporary focus time or sick leave.

A friend can check whether food is available without requiring conversation.

A relative can collect medication.

A clinician may already have your symptom history.

Write the plan with the people involved. Do not assume they will remember a conversation held months earlier.

The agreement should name action and duration.

"When I send the word amber, please take full responsibility for dinner and school messages for three days. Ask only urgent yes or no questions after work."

If someone refuses to participate, the prevention system needs another route. A plan is not real when it depends on support that has never been agreed.

Protect Recovery Access as Infrastructure

Recovery is commonly treated as what happens after all important work is complete. That position guarantees it will be removed first.

Treat some Recovery Access as infrastructure.

A protected evening.

One morning without appointments.

A quiet workspace.

Food that remains available.

An automatic reply.

A weekly period when another person owns caregiving.

Time with an interest.

The exact form depends on your life. Infrastructure is the support that keeps the rest of the system usable.

A road is not a reward for completing the journey. It is how movement remains possible. Recovery Access serves the same role.

Do not wait until every demand agrees that you deserve it.

Review Major Changes

Burnout risk changes when the system changes.

Review the plan after any of the following.

A job change

Medication change

Pregnancy or postpartum period

Perimenopause or menopause changes

Illness or injury

Relationship change

Move or housing change

New caregiving responsibility

Loss or bereavement

A diagnosis or new understanding of support needs

The old warning signs may shift. A new role may hide burnout through excitement for several months. A quieter home may reveal that work was the main source. A medication change may alter initiation, sleep, appetite, or daily timing, which can change how other support needs are experienced.

The plan should follow your current life, not preserve an old explanation.

Measure Sustainability, Not Maximum Output

Many systems measure what you completed. A prevention system also measures what remained available.

Did you eat?

Could you sleep?

Was speech available at home?

Could you tolerate ordinary input?

Did one difficult day require one night of recovery or an entire week?

Could you do something you valued that was not required?

A week of high output and total private collapse is not a stable green week.

A lower output week with reliable basic care, work, and some pleasure may be more sustainable.

This can be difficult to accept in workplaces and families that reward visible production. Your prevention system is allowed to count what they ignore.

A life is not sustainable because the deadline was met.

Expect False Alarms

Sometimes you will reduce demand and discover that the crash did not arrive. You may conclude that you overreacted.

The reduction may be why the crash did not arrive.

Prevention creates a strange evidence problem. When it works, the event you feared is absent. You cannot know with certainty what would have happened.

Use proportionate responses. Amber does not require abandoning your life. It requires a temporary, defined reduction while you watch the pattern.

If the signs pass, return gradually. If they remain, deepen support or seek assessment.

A false alarm that costs one cancelled plan may be preferable to certainty purchased through severe collapse.

Write the Personal Burnout Response Plan

Your plan should fit on two pages.

Page one contains:

Green, amber, and red signs

The threshold that opens amber

The Minimum Viable Day

Medical and urgent help indicators

Page two contains:

Tasks that reduce at amber

Tasks that transfer at red

People and services to contact

Saved messages

Recovery conditions

The first date for review

Keep the plan where you can find it. Share only the parts each person needs.

The plan is not proof that you can manage burnout alone. It is a bridge to support when thinking, speech, and decisions become less available.

Prepare a Burnout Support Kit

A support kit gathers the items and words that become difficult to find during decline.

It may contain safe foods, hydration options, ear protection, comfortable clothing, medication information, chargers, hygiene supplies, a small amount of emergency cash if safe, contact details, and printed copies of saved messages.

Digital versions can sit in one phone folder. Paper versions can help when screens are intolerable or a device is lost.

The kit should match your real needs. Do not buy a collection of products because they are marketed as regulating. Use items you already know are tolerable and useful.

Review dates and supplies every few months. A kit with expired food, old medication information, and a disconnected contact creates false reassurance.

Plan for Seasonal Pressure

Some load returns at predictable times: school holidays, tax deadlines, winter darkness, summer heat, annual reporting, religious events, family celebrations, travel seasons, or anniversaries.

Add these periods to the yearly map. Decide which support begins before the pressure rises.

You might reduce social commitments during annual reporting, prepare sensory support for hot weather, arrange childcare earlier, or simplify celebrations before invitations are accepted.

Seasonal planning does not mean expecting disaster. It means respecting patterns that have repeated.

Review the Near Miss

A near miss is a period when warning signs rose but severe collapse did not follow.

Review it without deciding whether you were "really" burnt out.

What signs appeared?

What changed?

Which support helped?

Which demand disappeared by chance?

What should become part of the permanent plan?

Near misses contain prevention data. They show which levers can close the gap before red.

Let the Plan Be Used by Others

During red periods, you may not be able to explain the plan. Give trusted people the part they need in advance.

A partner needs the household transfer list. A manager needs the work message. A friend needs the check-in agreement. A clinician needs the symptom and medication page.

Nobody needs every private detail.

A usable plan distributes action without distributing your entire history.

Practice the Plan While Green

A prevention plan is hardest to use for the first time during a red period. Test the parts while your access is better.

Send one saved message to yourself and check whether it says enough. Show a trusted person the responsibility list and ask what would be unclear during a crisis. Find the supplies in the support kit without searching the whole house. Open the document on your phone. Check whether the workplace contact and medical information are current.

This is not a rehearsal for disaster. It is a usability test. A plan that depends on memory, long explanations, several passwords, or one unavailable person may fail when you need it.

Zoe discovered that her written plan told her partner to "reduce demands" but did not name a single task. They replaced the phrase with three actions: take over dinner decisions, cancel nonessential visitors, and handle school messages for seven days. The revised plan removed interpretation at the point when neither of them had much capacity for it.

Keep the test brief. Fix one obstacle. Prevention becomes more reliable when the plan has already been opened, understood, and used once.

Use This Before the Crash

The Early Warning Window begins before your worst symptoms.

Use observable signs across body, thinking, sensory tolerance, communication, and daily living.

A green, amber, and red system reduces decisions during decline.

The weekly Capacity Gap Map should take five minutes and lead to one lever.

Prevention agreements must name who does what and for how long.

Recovery Access is infrastructure, not a reward left until everything else is complete.

Review the plan after major changes in health, work, hormones, relationships, housing, or responsibility.

Measure what remained available, not only what you produced.

The earlier response is allowed to look unnecessary because it worked.

Conclusion A Life Without Repeated Collapse

There may be a version of recovery you have been waiting for.

In that version, energy returns and stays. The house becomes manageable. Work no longer follows you into the evening. Noise stops hurting. Messages are easy again. You can make plans without calculating the cost. Nobody needs to adjust. You resume the life you had before and finally perform it correctly.

That version may not be the most useful target.

Recovery can include real improvement. Speech may return. Food may become easier. Sleep may settle. You may work, connect, create, travel, parent, study, exercise, or take on demanding projects again. The aim of this book has never been to convince you that a small life is the only safe one.

The aim is to stop using repeated collapse as the price of a meaningful life.

A life your brain can sustain may contain variation. Some weeks will cost more. Some environments will require support. Hormonal change, illness, grief, work, money, caregiving, and ordinary unpredictability will affect Available Capacity. A prevention plan cannot make those facts disappear.

It can change how long you wait before responding.

You now have language for the difference between ability and access. You can complete a task and still ask whether the task was recoverable and repeatable. You can notice the delayed bill instead of using the successful moment as proof that no cost existed.

You have the Capacity Gap Map. Visible Load tells you what the week asks. Hidden Load tells you what the task requires beneath its name. Available Capacity tells you what can be reached today. Recovery Access tells you whether the conditions for restoration actually exist.

The map does not issue a verdict. It gives you four levers.

Reduce load.

Reveal Hidden Load.

Add practical support.

Protect Recovery Access.

You will not always be able to reach the lever you need most. A job may remain inflexible. Money may restrict support. A relationship may refuse fair change. A health system may move slowly. The map is still useful because it stops locating every failure inside you.

Sometimes the gap is structural.

Sometimes the honest answer is that the current life asks more than the available support can sustain.

That recognition can be painful. It can also end the endless search for a planner, routine, supplement, morning practice, or burst of discipline that will make an impossible total feel ordinary.

Keep the Minimum Available

The Minimum Viable Day is not meant to become your permanent horizon. It is meant to remain available when severe periods return.

You know which essentials protect health, safety, housing, income, dependents, and basic care. You know that food can have a minimum version. Hygiene can have a supported version. Communication can use saved words. A task can transfer fully rather than waiting for you to direct it.

These are not signs that you have stopped trying.

They are evidence that your plan includes the person you become when access narrows.

Many systems are built for the person who can remember, choose, begin, sequence, tolerate, and recover. A reliable system includes the day when one or more of those functions is missing.

The system should not punish the person it was designed to support.

Let Support Remove Work

You may remember one distinction more than any other in the relationship chapters: help and ownership are not the same.

Support removes effort when another person notices, plans, remembers, completes, checks, and repairs. A task has not transferred if you still carry it mentally.

This applies beyond the household. A manager who agrees you are overwhelmed but keeps priorities vague has offered concern without reducing load. A friend who says “contact me if you need anything” may be sincere while leaving every initiation decision with you. A clinician who gives a long list of healthy actions without asking which functions are accessible may add treatment-related demands to the problem.

You can ask for support in observable terms.

One written instruction.

One meal decided and provided.

One period without questions.

One appointment booked.

One domain fully owned.

One meeting removed.

Specific support is easier to accept, provide, and assess.

Keep Pleasure in the Plan

Burnout recovery can become a life organized entirely around prevention.

You avoid noise, crowds, change, commitment, conflict, effort, and risk. The plan becomes efficient. It may also become empty.

Interest, connection, pleasure, humor, competence, movement, creativity, and chosen stimulation are not luxuries that must wait until the final stage. They are part of the reason you are protecting capacity.

Some pleasures cost energy. That does not make them mistakes.

The Capacity Gap Map allows you to plan for the cost instead of pretending it does not exist. Leave earlier. Protect the next morning. Choose the smaller group. Bring food. Use ear protection. Ask for direct information. Make the event less expensive without requiring it to become free.

A sustainable life contains effort you chose because something mattered.

Do Not Turn Insight Into Another Demand

You may finish this book with several useful changes in mind. That can create a familiar urge to do everything now.

Redesign the house. Speak with the manager. Transfer household domains. Build the Rest Menu. Track hormones. Contact the doctor. Reduce masking. Create the Return-to-Demand Ladder. Explain burnout to the family. Write the prevention plan.

That list can recreate the problem the book was meant to reduce.

Choose one change with a repeated effect.

Perhaps you protect the first 30 minutes after work.

Perhaps dinner becomes another person's responsibility.

Perhaps you prepare the medical appointment page.

Perhaps you reduce one recurring meeting.

Perhaps you create three zero energy rest options.

Perhaps you define the three signs that open your amber plan.

A repeated small reduction can change the week more than a large one time effort.

Recovery Is Not a Return Test

You may not return to the exact person you were before burnout.

That person may have been operating through urgency, fear, masking, skipped needs, and invisible recovery. She may have achieved things you value. She may also have paid in ways nobody saw.

You do not need to reject her.

You can thank the strategies that worked and stop requiring them to fund the future.

Recovery is not proved by tolerating the same environment again. It is not proved by removing every accommodation, resuming full hours, attending every event, or becoming easy for other people to understand.

Recovery is visible when life becomes more usable.

Food remains available.

Speech returns after work.

A difficult day no longer consumes the week.

You can ask for a change before a crisis.

You can enjoy something without spending the next two days in punishment.

You can notice the Early Warning Window and respond while choice remains.

You can make a plan from your actual capacity rather than the person you think you must perform.

Choose the Permanent Change

The final action in this book is small and serious.

Choose one change that will remain after the immediate burnout period improves.

Not a temporary rescue. A permanent correction to the old operating model.

It may be a morning without meetings, a workspace with less stimulation, a household responsibility that never returns to you, a repeated meal option, a protected recovery period, a shorter social commitment, a different standard for replies, a medication review, or a rule that the first good day is never used to catch up completely.

Write the change as one sentence:

"Even when I feel better, I will continue to __________ because __________."

Tell the person who needs to know. Put the support in the calendar, home, workplace, or relationship where it can survive your next burst of energy.

A permanent change is how recovery stops becoming a brief pause before the same conditions resume.

You are not trying to become a person who never needs support.

You are building a life in which support arrives before collapse has to prove the need.

Appendix A Capacity Gap Map

Use this page for a day, week, project, job, or life period. Keep the first version brief.

Visible Load

Write the demands that are easy to name.
Paid work:

Caregiving:

Household:

Health and appointments:

Travel:

Money and administration:

Social commitments:

Other fixed demands:

Hidden Load

Write the work beneath the task.
Masking and social monitoring:

Sensory filtering:

Preparation and rehearsal:

Switching and interruption:

Uncertainty and waiting:

Emotional monitoring:

Pain, sleep loss, or physical strain:

Recovery required afterward:

Available Capacity

Mark each as higher, mixed, or lower.
Thinking and decisions:

Starting and switching:

Sensory tolerance:

Speech and social contact:

Physical energy:

Daily living:

Mood and interest:

Recovery Access

Time genuinely protected:

Privacy:

Control over sound, light, touch, temperature, and movement:

Freedom from work contact:

Freedom from caregiving or household responsibility:

Practical support:

Suitable rest and interest:

Main barrier to recovery:

Choose One Lever

Load to reduce:

Hidden Load to reveal:

Support to add:

Recovery condition to protect:

One change for the next seven days:

Appendix B Minimum Viable Day

A Minimum Viable Day protects the smallest safe version of life during severe burnout.

If food, essential medication, dependent care, housing, or safety cannot be maintained, seek practical or professional help rather than relying on this worksheet alone.

Essential Outcomes

Medication or treatment:

Food and drink:

Dependent care:

Housing or income task:

Urgent communication:

Safety:

Minimum Versions

Food:

Hygiene:

Clothing:

Medication:

Work or study:

Caregiving:

Communication:

Household:

Tasks That Pause

Delayable:

Delegable:

Removable:

One Recovery Condition

For the next ______ days, I need:

One Support Request

Person or service:

Exact task they will own:

Duration:

Appendix C Rest Menu

Choose options based on current Available Capacity. Remove anything that creates pressure or does not suit your health and circumstances.

Zero Energy

Option one:

Option two:

Option three:

Chosen sound or silence:

Chosen light:

Body support:

Low language contact:

Low Energy

Option one:

Option two:

Option three:

Familiar interest:

Gentle movement if suitable:

Quiet company:

Moderate Energy

Option one:

Option two:

Option three:

Connection:

Time outside:

Creative or focused interest:

Afterward Check

Speech access: less available, unchanged, or more available

Decision access: less available, unchanged, or more available

Sensory tolerance: lower, unchanged, or higher

Body tension: higher, unchanged, or lower

Access to one basic task: less available, unchanged, or more available

Appendix D Medical Appointment Page

This page helps organize concerns. It does not tell a clinician what diagnosis to make.

Main Concern

My main concern is:

It began or changed around:

It affects daily life by:

Pattern

Physical energy:

Sleep:

Mood and interest:

Sensory tolerance:

Thinking and memory:

Speech and communication:

Food and appetite:

Pain or other physical symptoms:

Menstrual or hormonal pattern, if relevant:

Recent infection, illness, pregnancy, medication change, or major event:

Medication

Name and dose:

Timing:

Benefits:

Unwanted effects:

What happens as it wears off:

Questions

Could more than one condition be contributing?
What alternatives should be considered?
What tests, assessment, or follow-up are appropriate?
What changes should prompt urgent review?
When should I return if this does not improve?

Appendix E Work Adjustment Request

Use local employment advice when legal rights, disclosure, or documentation matter.

The Barrier

The current barrier is:

Work Effect

It affects my work by:

Requested Change

I am requesting:

Useful Outcome

This would support the role by:

Trial and Review

We can test this for:

We can review it through:

Example

The current barrier is frequent unplanned interruption during technical work. It creates repeated restart time and avoidable errors. I am requesting two protected focus blocks each day with messages paused except for urgent issues. This would support accurate completion of the monthly report. We can test it for four weeks and review completion times and error corrections.

Appendix F Support Agreement

Early Signs

The first changes you may notice are:

Overload Signal

The word, message, or action I will use is:

It means:

What Helps

Please:

What Makes It Worse

Please avoid:

Responsibilities That Transfer

Task or domain:

Owner:

Duration:

Low Language Plan

If speech is limited, I can answer:

Yes or no questions
Written questions
No questions for ______ minutes

Another agreed format:

Review Date

We will review this plan on:

Appendix G Capacity Tracker for Eight Weeks

Record only the fields that are useful. A shorter tracker completed regularly is enough.
Date:

Cycle day or hormonal stage, if relevant:

Sleep: higher, mixed, or lower
Perceived medication benefit: higher, mixed, or lower
Unwanted effects or concerns:

Sensory tolerance: higher, mixed, or lower
Starting and switching: higher, mixed, or lower
Mood and interest: higher, mixed, or lower
Speech and social tolerance: higher, mixed, or lower
Food access: higher, mixed, or lower
Pain or physical symptoms:

Major demands:

Delayed cost from the previous day:

Appendix H Return-to-Demand Ladder

Choose one domain such as work, social life, household, study, exercise, or caregiving.

This is a practical pacing worksheet, not a medical rehabilitation protocol. Seek professional advice if activity causes delayed or medically concerning worsening.

Capacity Floor

The five functions I will protect are:

1.
2.
3.
4.
5.

Stage One

Familiar, low uncertainty, low social demand, easy to stop:

Recovery condition:

Review date:

Stage Two

Longer duration or moderate complexity:

Recovery condition:

Review date:

Stage Three

Increased frequency, social demand, travel, or uncertainty:

Recovery condition:

Review date:

Stage Four

High consequence or high complexity demand:

Recovery condition:

Review date:

Step Down Rule

If these floor functions become strained or lost:

I will return to stage:

Appendix I Burnout Response Plan

This is a personal planning tool, not a diagnostic or emergency triage scale. Follow local emergency guidance when safety or urgent medical concerns arise.

Green

My stable signs are:

Supports that remain in place:

Amber

My early warning signs are:

My amber threshold is:

When amber begins, I reduce:

I transfer:

I protect:

I contact:

Red

My severe signs are:

My Minimum Viable Day is:

The responsibilities that transfer are:

The professional or urgent help indicators are:

People or services to contact:

Saved Messages

Work:

Family:

Friend:

Medical:

Review

Next review date:

Major changes that require an earlier review:

References

Ali, D., Bougoure, M., Cooper, B., Quinton, A. M. G., Tan, D., Brett, J., Mandy, W., Maybery, M., Magiati, I., & Happé, F. (2025). Burnout as experienced by autistic people: A systematic review. *Clinical Psychology Review, 122*, Article 102669. https://doi.org/10.1016/j.cpr.2025.102669

Arnold, S. R. C., Higgins, J. M., Weise, J., Desai, A., Pellicano, E., & Trollor, J. N. (2023). Towards the measurement of autistic burnout. *Autism, 27*(7), 1933-1948. https://doi.org/10.1177/13623613221147401

Bougoure, M., Zhuang, S., Brett, J. D., Maybery, M. T., English, M. C., Tan, D. W., & Magiati, I. (2026). Measuring autistic burnout: A psychometric validation of the AASPIRE Autistic Burnout Measure in autistic adults. *Autism, 30*(1), 20-36. https://doi.org/10.1177/13623613251355255

Bradley, L., Shaw, R., Baron-Cohen, S., & Cassidy, S. (2021). Autistic adults' experiences of camouflaging and its perceived impact on mental health. *Autism in Adulthood, 3*(4), 320-329. https://doi.org/10.1089/aut.2020.0071

Cage, E., & Troxell-Whitman, Z. (2019). Understanding the reasons, contexts and costs of camouflaging for autistic adults. *Journal of Autism and Developmental Disorders, 49*(5), 1899-1911. https://doi.org/10.1007/s10803-018-03878-x

Craddock, E. (2024). Being a woman is 100% significant to my experiences of attention deficit hyperactivity disorder and autism: Exploring the gendered implications of an adulthood combined autism and attention deficit hyperactivity disorder diagnosis. *Qualitative Health Research, 34*(14), 1442-1455. https://doi.org/10.1177/10497323241253412

Craddock, E. (2026). Navigating residual diagnostic categories: The lived experiences of women diagnosed with autism and ADHD in adulthood. *Health, 30*(2), 235-257. https://doi.org/10.1177/13634593251336163

Eng, A. G., Nirjar, U., Elkins, A. R., Sizemore, Y. J., Monticello, K. N., Petersen, M. K., Miller, S. A., Barone, J., Eisenlohr-Moul, T. A., & Martel, M. M. (2024). Attention deficit hyperactivity disorder and the menstrual cycle: Theory and evidence. *Hormones and Behavior, 158*, Article 105466. https://doi.org/10.1016/j.yhbeh.2023.105466

Evans, J. A., Krumrei-Mancuso, E. J., & Rouse, S. V. (2024). What you are hiding could be hurting you: Autistic masking in relation to mental health, interpersonal trauma, authenticity, and self-esteem. *Autism in Adulthood, 6*(2), 229-240. https://doi.org/10.1089/aut.2022.0115

Findeis, H., & Strauß, M. (2025). The effects of psychostimulants in menstruating women with ADHD: A gender health gap in ADHD treatment? *Progress in Neuro-Psychopharmacology and Biological Psychiatry, 137*, Article 111261. https://doi.org/10.1016/j.pnpbp.2025.111261

Gottardello, D., & Steffan, B. (2024). Fundamental intersectionality of menopause and neurodivergence experiences at work. *Maturitas, 189*, Article 108107. https://doi.org/10.1016/j.maturitas.2024.108107

Grove, R., Hoekstra, R. A., Wierda, M., & Begeer, S. (2018). Special interests and subjective wellbeing in autistic adults. *Autism Research, 11*(5), 766-775. https://doi.org/10.1002/aur.1931

Hull, L., Petrides, K. V., Allison, C., Smith, P., Baron-Cohen, S., Lai, M.-C., & Mandy, W. (2017). "Putting on my best normal": Social camouflaging in adults with autism spectrum conditions. *Journal of Autism and Developmental Disorders, 47*(8), 2519-2534. https://doi.org/10.1007/s10803-017-3166-5

Khalifa, G., Sharif, Z., Sultan, M., & Di Rezze, B. (2020). Workplace accommodations for adults with autism spectrum disorder: A scoping review. *Disability and Rehabilitation, 42*(9), 1316-1331. https://doi.org/10.1080/09638288.2018.1527952

Klein, J., Krahn, R., Howe, S., Lewis, J., McMorris, C., & Macoun, S. (2025). A systematic review of social camouflaging in autistic adults and youth: Implications and theory. *Development and Psychopathology, 37*(3), 1320-1334. https://doi.org/10.1017/S0954579424001159

Lewis, L. F., & Stevens, K. (2023). The lived experience of meltdowns for autistic adults. *Autism, 27*(6), 1817-1825. https://doi.org/10.1177/13623613221145783

Lindsay, S., Osten, V., Rezai, M., & Bui, S. (2021). Disclosure and workplace accommodations for people with autism: A systematic review. *Disability and Rehabilitation, 43*(5), 597-610. https://doi.org/10.1080/09638288.2019.1635658

Mantzalas, J., Richdale, A. L., Adikari, A., Lowe, J., & Dissanayake, C. (2022). What is autistic burnout? A thematic analysis of posts on two online platforms. *Autism in Adulthood, 4*(1), 52-65. https://doi.org/10.1089/aut.2021.0021

National Health Service. (2022). *Get help with low mood, sadness or depression.* https://www.nhs.uk/mental-health/feelings-symptoms-behaviours/feelings-and-symptoms/low-mood-sadness-depression/

National Health Service. (2023a). *Postpartum psychosis.* https://www.nhs.uk/mental-health/conditions/post-partum-psychosis/

National Health Service. (2023b). *Problems swallowing pills.* https://www.nhs.uk/conditions/problems-swallowing-pills/

National Health Service. (2023c). *Tiredness and fatigue.* https://www.nhs.uk/symptoms/tiredness-and-fatigue/

National Health Service. (2024a). *Myalgic encephalomyelitis or chronic fatigue syndrome (ME/CFS)*. https://www.nhs.uk/conditions/chronic-fatigue-syndrome-cfs/

National Health Service. (2024b). *Shortness of breath*. https://www.nhs.uk/symptoms/shortness-of-breath/

National Health Service. (2024c). *Sudden confusion (delirium)*. https://www.nhs.uk/symptoms/confusion/

National Health Service. (2026a). *Postnatal depression*. https://www.nhs.uk/mental-health/conditions/postnatal-depression/

National Health Service. (2026b). *Symptoms of menopause and perimenopause*. https://www.nhs.uk/conditions/menopause-and-perimenopause/symptoms/

National Institute for Health and Care Excellence. (2018). *Attention deficit hyperactivity disorder: Diagnosis and management* (NICE Guideline NG87). https://www.nice.org.uk/guidance/ng87

Osianlis, E., Thomas, E. H. X., Jenkins, L. M., & Gurvich, C. (2025). ADHD and sex hormones in females: A systematic review. *Journal of Attention Disorders, 29*(9), 706-723. https://doi.org/10.1177/10870547251332319

Paris, K., Lodestone, A. Z., Houser, M., & Lewis, L. F. (2025). “Shutdowns are like you’re stuck on the blue screen of death”: A metaphor analysis of autistic shutdowns. *Autism in Adulthood*. Advance online publication. https://doi.org/10.1089/aut.2024.0193

Petty, S., Tunstall, L., Richardson, H., & Eccles, N. (2023). Workplace adjustments for autistic employees: What is ‘reasonable’? *Journal of Autism and Developmental Disorders, 53*(1), 236-244. https://doi.org/10.1007/s10803-021-05413-x

Rapoport, I. L., & Groenman, A. P. (2025). A review of sex and gender factors in stimulant treatment for ADHD: Knowledge gaps and future directions. *Journal of Attention Disorders, 29*(8), 602-616. https://doi.org/10.1177/10870547251315601

Raymaker, D. M., Teo, A. R., Steckler, N. A., Lentz, B., Scharer, M., Delos Santos, A., Kapp, S. K., Hunter, M., Joyce, A., & Nicolaidis, C. (2020). "Having all of your internal resources exhausted beyond measure and being left with no clean-up crew": Defining autistic burnout. *Autism in Adulthood, 2*(2), 132-143. https://doi.org/10.1089/aut.2019.0079

Tamura, M., Cage, E., Perry, E., Hongo, M., Takahashi, T., Seto, M., Shimizu, E., & Oshima, F. (2025). Understanding camouflaging, stigma, and mental health for autistic people in Japan. *Autism in Adulthood, 7*(1), 52-65. https://doi.org/10.1089/aut.2023.0035

Wynchank, D., Sutrisno, R. M. G. T. M. F., van Andel, E., & Kooij, J. J. S. (2026). Menstrual cycle related hormonal fluctuations in ADHD: Effect on cognitive functioning, a narrative review. *Journal of Clinical Medicine, 15*(1), Article 121. https://doi.org/10.3390/jcm15010121

www.ingramcontent.com/pod-product-compliance
Lightning Source LLC
LaVergne TN
LVHW010724061126
851857LV00014B/1334